VIRTUAL THEATRES

Virtual Theatres presents the theatre of the twenty-first century in which everything – even the viewer – can be simulated. In this fascinating volume, Gabriella Giannachi analyses the aesthetic concerns of current computer-arts practices through a discussion of a variety of artists and performers including

- Blast Theory
- Merce Cunningham
- Eduardo Kac
- Forced Entertainment
- Lynn Hershman
- Jodi
- Orlan
- Guillermo Gómez-Peña
- Marcel-lí Antúnez Roca
- Jeffrey Shaw
- Stelarc.

This is the first full-length book of its kind to offer an investigation of the interface between theatre, performance and digital arts. *Virtual Theatres* not only allows for a reinterpretation of what is possible in the world of performance practice, but also demonstrates how 'virtuality' has come to represent a major parameter for our understanding and experience of contemporary art and life.

Gabriella Giannachi is a lecturer in Theatre Studies at the University of Lancaster, where her specialist areas include new technologies and performance. She is also co-editor of *On Directing* (1999) and co-author of *Staging the Post-Avant-Garde* (2002).

VIRTUAL THEATRES

An introduction

Gabriella Giannachi

Routledge
Taylor & Francis Group

LONDON AND NEW YORK

First published 2004
by Routledge
11 New Fetter Lane, London EC4P 4EE

Simultaneously published in the USA and Canada
by Routledge
29 West 35th Street, New York, NY 10001

Routledge is an imprint of the Taylor & Francis Group

© 2004 Gabriella Giannachi

Typeset in Bembo by
Florence Production Ltd, Stoodleigh, Devon
Printed and bound in Great Britain by
TJ International Ltd, Padstow, Cornwall

British Library Cataloguing in Publication Data
A catalogue record for this book is available from the British Library

Library of Congress Cataloging in Publication Data
Giannachi, Gabriella.
Virtual theatres : an introduction / Gabriella Giannachi.
p. cm.
Includes bibliographical references and index.
1. Experimental theater. 2. Virtual reality. I. Title.
PN2193.E86G53 2004
792.02′2–dc22   2003018855

ISBN 0–415–28378–7 (hbk)
ISBN 0–415–28379–5 (pbk)

TO NICK

CONTENTS

ILLUSTRATIONS

ACKNOWLEDGEMENTS

Virtual Theatres has been developed with the support of a number of individuals whose advice has been essential in the completion of this book. First, thanks are due to Dr Benjamin Macias, who drew my attention to the subject over ten years ago. I would also like to thank Stelarc for the unfailing enthusiasm with which he explained his work in a long and essential interview. Moreover, the assistance of Professor Nick Kaye, Dr Kate Newey, Dr Andrew Quick, Jennifer Sheridan and Nigel Stewart has been invaluable in identifying indispensable materials, while Professor Peter Holland and Professor David Thomas were supportive of the project in its early days. I am similarly indebted to Professor Mel Slater and, especially, Dr David Swapp from the Department of Computer Science at University College, London, for allowing me to visit their CAVE, and to the staff from the archive at ZKM in Karlsruhe for their assistance in locating important texts. I am also grateful to the personnel at the Ars Electronica Centre in Linz for their enthusiastic demonstrations of the artworks, and the staff of Futurelab, especially to Mag. Romana Staufer, who made my access to the archives possible, and to Michaela Wimplinger, who helped with the practicalities. Moreover, I would like to thank the staff at V2 in Rotterdam, especially Sandra 'Fokky' Fauconnier, who assisted me in locating crucial material for this book.

This project has received significant institutional support that has been essential to its completion. Most importantly, I would like to thank the Arts and Humanities Research Board for offering substantial financial support for research travel to essential archives and sites in Germany, Holland and Austria. I am also indebted to the Arts and Humanities Research Board for granting a research leave award which undoubtedly facilitated the completion of this book. The University of Lancaster and my colleagues provided additional support to the project through an important period of sabbatical leave. Moreover, I

ACKNOWLEDGEMENTS

am grateful to Rosie Waters, who commissioned the book, and Talia Rodgers and Diane Parker who saw it to completion. I am also, as always, indebted to my parents, Lieselotte Mangels Giannachi and Bruno Giannachi, for their love, friendship and support. Last, but not least, I would like to acknowledge my considerable debt to Nick Kaye for his ongoing support, unfailing encouragement and general advice. To him I am particularly indebted for a very stimulating exchange of ideas that informed all stages of the work. Many of these conversations took place in the company of our baby daughter Francesca, who was born nearly halfway through the writing of this book and whose smiles and first attempts at communication have helped me to see beyond it. Like everything else I do, this book is also for her.

Finally, I am pleased to acknowledge the kind permission of the following individuals and companies to reproduce the illustrations that make a vital contribution to this volume: the cover image *Liquid Views – Liquid People* by kind permission of Monika Fleischmann and Wolfgang Strauss; Figures 1 and 2 by kind permission of 0100101110101101.ORG; Figure 3 by kind permission of Jeffrey Shaw and ZKM, Centre for Art and Media, Karlsruhe; Figure 4 by kind permission of Masaki Fujihata; Figure 5 by kind permission of Tim Etchells, Hugo Glendinning and Forced Entertainment; Figure 6 by kind permission of Stelarc; Figure 7 by kind permission of Marcellí Antúnez Roca; Figure 8 by kind permission of Christa Sommerer and Laurent Mignonneau; Figure 9 by kind permission of Eduardo Kac and Julia Friedman; Figure 10 by kind permission of Nox; Figure 11 by kind permission of Paul Sermon; Figure 12 by kind permission of Blast Theory; Figure 13 by kind permission of the Merce Cunningham Dance Foundation; Figure 14 by kind permission of Maurice Benayoun; Figure 15 by kind permission of Lynn Hershman; Figure 16 by kind permission of La Pocha Nostra; Figure 17 by kind permission of Jeffrey Shaw and ZKM, Centre for Art and Media, Karlsruhe; and Figure 18 by kind permission of Tamás Waliczky.

All translations specifically for this volume are by myself.

INTRODUCTION

Technology and art

The etymology of the word 'technology', *tekhnē*, indicates that technology is also an art, a craft, and shows how profoundly technology and art are linked. Just as art has repeatedly advanced through technology, technology has, via art, acquired aesthetic signification. In the early twentieth century a movement evolved which not only made innovative use of technology in art, but also for the first time gave serious consideration to technology as a *form* of art. This movement derived from the First World War and was characterised by an obsession with mechanics across all arts, most importantly in Vsevolod Meyerhold's work with biomechanics, which in many ways represented a theatrical attempt to create a meeting-ground for the interplay of biology and technology. Likewise, with Oscar Schlemmer's 'puppets', the body was transformed into a machine through the use of stage costume composed of a mechanised system of parts. Here, dancers pursued precise series of kinematic sequences which followed the design of the costume and the structure of the piece. In Schlemmer's work, 'the body that appears on stage is a body *extended through space*, a body where costume and scenery merge, where anatomic and spatial geometric forms become a single form of nature and culture' (Palumbo 2000: 19, original emphasis). This architectural biomechanical body of the Bauhaus was therefore literally 'extended through space' (*ibid.*: 16) and in many ways represented a theatrical proto-cyborg. As Sue-Ellen Case points out, this body, wearing geometric designs, and literally extending 'its gestures outward, through poles' resembled the image of the computer mouse as an extension of the arm (Case 1996: 94), which transforms today's computer-user into a cyborg.

But Bauhaus was not the only avant-garde movement interested in experimentation with technology. Dada, especially through Francis

INTRODUCTION

Picabia, who identified the machine as 'the genius of the modern world' (Picabia in Popper 1993: 11), and Constructivism were equally important in promulgating the role of technology within art. Likewise, Cubism, which had grown out of an 'increasing sense of urban dynamism and the inability of the painter to register the relativity of object–observer movements with the traditional tools of representation' (Burnham 1968: 206), and Futurism, with Filippo Tommaso Marinetti's exaltation of the machine, were both revolutionary in presenting technology as the means to move forward within aesthetic discourse. Then there was Bertolt Brecht's enthusiasm for science and technology as tools towards the realisation of a Marxist society and hence instruments, in theatre and life, towards the actualisation of progress. Indeed, even before the robot was introduced in Karel Čapek's play *R.U.R.* in 1923, works presenting figures that resembled robots appeared in paintings by Kasimir Malevich and Fernand Léger, whose *The Card Players* (1917) 'most precisely defines the robot in modern form' (*ibid.*: 210). Later machine works were created by Francis Picabia and Marcel Duchamp, although it was not until the second half of the twentieth century that 'the machine overtly entered the iconography of art' (*ibid.*: 211). Picabia suggested a 'certain merging of interests and physical characteristics between machines and future human beings' (*ibid.*: 211), a statement that is still at the heart of the contemporary debate about the cyborg. Photography, of course, also played a major role in the synthesis of art and technology, and such pieces as Etienne-Jules Marey's *Gymnast Jumping over a Chair* (1883) and Eadweard Muybridge's *Ascending and Descending Stairs* and *Descending Stairs and Turning Around*, from the series *Animal Locomotion* (1884–5), drew attention to kinetics and the organisation of time and space in art through technology. Finally, experimental cinema was also crucial in furthering the collaboration between art and technology, especially in works such as Sergei Eisenstein's *The Battleship Potemkin* (1925) and Dziga Vertov's *The Man with the Movie Camera* (1929).

These avant-garde movements and their passionate belief in technology were inspirational to experimental art and performance in the 1960s and 1970s. Especially important were the works of Duchamp, Alexander Calder and Jean Tinguely, as well as those of Man Ray, Lásló Moholy-Nagy and Vladimir Tatlin, who were highly significant in laying the groundwork for the investigation into the interrelatedness of art and technology. The origins of robotic or cyborg art may be found in Kinetic Art work by Tinguely from the 1950s or Nam June Paik's robots and Bruce Lacey's automata from the 1960s. Frank

2

INTRODUCTION

Popper (1993) identifies a number of major influences on electronic art: namely, among others, photography and cinematography, conceptual and holographic art, Land Art, Light Art, Kinetic Art and Video Art. Being influenced by technology, however, has not always translated into a passion for technologies. Movements such as Fluxus, for instance, reacted against the machine by appropriating its products, 'displacing them from their everyday contexts, and "preparing" and maltreating them' (Huhtamo in Moser and MacLeod 1996: 237). On the other hand, John Cage and Merce Cunningham, with Robert Rauschenberg, Pop Art and especially Andy Warhol in his use of repetition, have introduced their audiences and viewers to revolutionary ways of looking at technology and art. Rauschenberg in particular was especially influential through his *Nine Evenings: Theater and Engineering* (1966) and the subsequent foundation, with Billie Klüver, of EAT (Experiments in Arts and Technology, 1967), which started an 'enduring and influential' collaboration between artists and engineers (Rush 1999: 38). Finally, works from expanded cinema and early video could be described as proto-virtual-reality experiments. This was especially the case for artists such as Nam June Paik, but also for Joan Jonas, Bruce Nauman, Vito Acconci, Dan Graham, Douglas Davis, Douglas Gordon, Gary Hill, Marina Abramovic, Laurie Anderson, Peter Campus, the Wooster Group, the Builders Association, Studio Azzurro and dumb type. Paik's *Video Synthesizer* (1969–70) even represented, in his opinion, the very 'beginning of the Internet' (Paik in Baumgärtel 2001: 40).

The first computers appeared in 1945, but initially were used solely by the military, with civilian use starting only in the 1960s. Roy Ascott pointed out the importance of cybernetics for the arts as early as 1966, and Jack Burnham introduced the concept of cyborg art a mere two years later (Dinkla 1997: 30). Meanwhile, Doug Engelbart, the inventor of the computer mouse, held a lecture at the Fall Joint Computer Conference in San Francisco in 1968 in which he demonstrated networked computers, video conferencing, hypermedia and hypertext (Weibel and Druckrey 2001: 19). Personal computers started to appear in 1975, and IBM announced its first model in 1981. In these years the development and commercialisation of the microprocessor gave rise to a new phase of industrial development which included robotics and automation (Lévy 2001: 13). The term 'cyberspace', however, was coined only in 1984, by William Gibson in his science-fiction novel *Neuromancer*. With this book, the long romance of fiction, art and technology became so consolidated that it is today hard to imagine that they could ever have been separate.

Cyberspace is a 'chaotic system' (Lévy 2001: 91), 'the *communications space made accessible through the global interconnection of computers and computer memories*' (*ibid*.: 74, original emphasis). One of the most important characteristics of cyberart is 'the participation in the work of those who experience, interpret, explore, or read it', which does not just amount to their participation in constructing meaning, 'but rather, their coproduction in the actual work' (*ibid*.: 116). The viewer not only participates in the production of the work, but does so in an open way. So cyberart is 'collective creation' in which the work has to be designed openly, '[t]hus creation is no longer limited to the moment of conception or realisation; the virtual system provides a machine for generating events' (*ibid*.: 116). In this context, Pierre Lévy identifies two major types of virtual world: 'those that are limited and editorialised, such as CD-ROMs and "closed" (off-line) installations by artists, [and] those that are accessible over a network and infinitely open to interaction, transformation, and connection with other virtual worlds (on-line)' (*ibid*.: 125–6). Lévy sees these two worlds as complementary to each other (*ibid*.: 126). Thus, although the virtual theatres described in this book are constituted by a variety of forms belonging to Lévy's categories, but also moving beyond them, they all share the characteristic of being open works in which the viewer is variously participating to the work of art from within it. This is why, in the world of virtual theatre, the work of art *and* the viewer are mediated. Hence, to understand the mechanisms at the heart of virtual theatre, it is necessary to understand the whole philosophical and material phenomenon of 'remediation'.

Remediation

Marshall McLuhan first drew attention to the role of mediation in contemporary society. Not only did he famously recognise that '[t]he medium is the message' (McLuhan 1987: 13) but that 'the "content" of any medium is always another medium' (*ibid*.: 8). The importance of this theory was recognised by Jay David Bolter and Richard Grusin, who expanded on McLuhan's claim in their book *Remediation* (2000), in which they argue that the main characteristic of digital media is its capacity to remediate, a phenomenon they define as the 'representation of one medium in another' (Bolter and Grusin 2000: 45). In their analysis, the medium itself is defined as that which remediates (*ibid*.: 19), so it is possible to conclude that, for them, all media remediate other media at the level of both content and form.

The first consequence of these assertions for a study of virtual theatre and performance is that any study of the phenomenon of virtuality from an aesthetic point of view has to take its mediatedness into account. It is therefore important to bear in mind both the role of the medium itself, and that it is the very use of the medium, including the role played in mediating the encounter between the viewer and the work of art, that determines the 'message', or content of the work. Second, it must be remembered that the medium itself always remediates. In relation to an analysis of virtual theatre and performance, this means that virtual theatre is therefore subject to a process not only of mediation but also of remediation. This implies the use of a certain degree of intertextuality and metatextuality, but also of intermediality and metamediality. In other words, the medium of virtual theatre is always also its content and this content is always also inclusive of other media. It is the very metadiscoursivity about these other media that allows the work to be metamedial – about media. Hence, virtual theatre is a form of theatre which remediates – which means that it is always also about media.

Virtual reality, one of the forms of virtual theatre analysed in this book, is, of course, also immersive: 'it is a medium whose purpose is to disappear' (Bolter and Grusin 2000: 21). Not only do 'programmers seek to remove the traces of their presence in order to give the program the greatest possible autonomy' (*ibid.*: 27), but also, unlike painting and figurative arts, the remediation is in itself subject to a process of disappearance. It is therefore possible to maintain that virtual theatre, whether through virtual reality or other forms of virtual performance, is created through a process of disappearance. This can be said not only because it involves a performative process which 'plunges into visibility' only to disappear again into memory (Phelan 1993: 148), but also because the medium itself operates by creating a flickering balance of appearance *and* disappearance. It is within this 'balance' that the viewer performs the work of art. And so, although the mediatised simulation is more or less reproducible, the viewer's performance of it is not.

The processes of appearance and disappearance that operate within the world of remediation are very complex. Philip Auslander first pointed to the fact that not only performance but also mediatised work are live and therefore subject to disappearance. Thus he showed that '[b]oth live performance and the performance of mediatization are predicated on disappearance: the televisual image is produced by an ongoing process in which scan lines replace one another and is always as absent as it is present; the use of recordings causes them to degenerate' (Auslander 1999: 45). He goes on to argue that 'the historical relationship of liveness and mediatization must be seen as a relation of dependence and imbrication rather than opposition' (*ibid.*: 53) and so 'the "live" can be defined only as "*that which can be recorded*"' (*ibid.*: 51, original emphasis), thus the medium disappears, deteriorates, as a result of its appearance, its happening. Similar conclusions had been reached by Sean Cubitt who showed that, in television,

> the broadcast flow is [. . .] a vanishing, a constant disappearing of what has just been shown. The elector scan builds up two images of each frame shown, the lines interlacing to form a 'complete' picture. Yet not only is the sensation of movement on screen an optical illusion brought about by the rapid succession of frames: each frame is itself radically incomplete, the line before always fading away, the first scan of the frame all but gone, even from the retina, before the second interlacing scan is complete [. . .] TV's presence to the viewer is subject to a constant flux: it is only intermittently 'present', as a kind of writing on the glass [. . .] caught in a dialectic of constant becoming and constant fading.
>
> (Cubitt 1991: 30–1)

But whereas virtual theatre's performative and remediated nature makes it subject to disappearance, the very fact that it is constituted by remediation also means that it must be read in terms of Paul Virilio's findings about the production of the information world, which, he claims, clearly privileges appearance, arrival:

> [f]ollowing the three phases of displacement – departure, journey, arrival – and after the demise of the 'journey', suddenly it is 'departure' that we have lost. From now on, *everything arrives* without our having to leave. But what 'arrives' is already no longer a stopover or the end of the trip; it is merely information, *information-world*, no, *information universe!*
>
> (Virilio 1996: 131–2, original emphases)

Thus, virtual theatre consists of a performative component, which is unique in time, and a remediated component, which is more or less permanent. This means that virtual theatre takes place through the viewer's 'performance' of the work and its disappearance into memory (of both the viewer and, on occasion, the work itself). However, this also means that, because virtual theatre takes place through a process of remediation, the environment in which the performance takes place is disappearing both in the sense that it is deteriorating *and* because it consists of a discontinuous, 'unreal' and yet live simulation. At the same time, its ability to remediate also suggests that virtual theatre is continuously (re-)arriving, (re)appearing as a fresh carnival of hyper-real signs.

As suggested by William Mitchell, '[a] digital image may be part scanned photograph, part computer-synthesised shaded perspective, and part electronic "painting" – all smoothly melded into an apparently coherent whole. It may be fabricated from found files, disk litter, the detritus of cyberspace' (Mitchell 1992: 78). In other words, the world that the virtual theatre user perceives as appearing around them is synthetic, made of text, mathematical formulae, not a proof, copy or representation of the real world. Thus the user is immersed in a world almost entirely made of what Jean Baudrillard defined as a new generation of signs and objects 'which will never have to be *counterfeits*, since from the outset they will be *products* on a gigantic scale' (Baudrillard 1998: 55, original emphases). So, although the virtual world is exclusively made of these new hypersigns, it is the viewer who constitutes the other, 'real' performance of virtual theatre.

But, in contrast to a traditional set or stage, the performer of virtual theatre is inside the work of art, not only metaphorically, but ontologically. In explaining the difference between the work of a painter and that of a cameraman, Walter Benjamin likened the painter to the magician and the cameraman to the surgeon. Whereas the magician, 'maintains the natural distance between the patient and himself', the surgeon 'does exactly the reverse; he greatly diminishes the distance between himself and the patient's body'; so, whereas the magician faces the patient 'man to man', the surgeon 'penetrates into him' (Benjamin 1992: 227). In other words, whereas '[t]he painter maintains in his work a natural distance from reality, the cameraman penetrates deeply into its web' (*ibid.*: 214). This analysis also applies to the making of virtual theatre. As suggested by Popper, 'a three-dimensional synthesis enables the artist to intervene not only on the image, but inside the image. Image has become architecture' (Popper 1993: 77), so the creation and the subsequent performance of the work takes place from within the world of the work. Moreover, as Virilio argues,

> [c]yberspace is a new form of perspective. It does not coin-
> cide with the audio-visual perspective which we already

know. It is a fully new perspective, free of any previous reference: it is a *tactile perspective*. To see at a distance, to hear at
a distance: that was the essence of the audio-visual perspective of old. But to reach at a distance, to feel at a distance,
that amounts to shifting the perspective towards a domain it
did not yet encompass: that of contact, of contact-at-a-
distance: tele-contact.

(Virilio 1995, original emphasis)

In cyberspace not only can the viewer feel at a distance, but they
can feel what in reality is not there: '[a] rock thrown at you in VR is
not a rock until it hits your head and hurts' (Stenslie in Beckmann
1998: 21). So even if virtual reality is not 'real', it still has to produce
a 'real' effect in the user. Therefore, not only is the viewer inside the
work of art, but they are operating it, possibly even modifying it, in
real time, and being modified by it in return. In this sense virtual
theatre remediates not only other media, but also the viewer's
performance. Baudrillard argues that modernity was the moment of
liberation and today all we can do is simulate the liberation
(Baudrillard 1993: 3). This is important when attempting to understand virtual theatre because it is not so much the place in which the
viewer is liberated from the canon and the dramaturgy of theatre arts
or even life, but the place where the viewer is continuously
performing the simulation of that liberation, and thereby continuously
re-enacting their own performance of the medium, creating an actual
theatre, a theatre of virtual reality, a theatre that must continuously
appear because it is always already *disappeared*.

The theatre of virtual reality

Brenda Laurel's *Computers as Theatre* (1993) was the first major study
to draw attention to the theatrical quality of human–computer interaction. Shortly thereafter, Jon McKenzie suggested that Laurel's
Aristotelian view of computers as theatre should be expanded to
include Bertolt Brecht, Antonin Artaud, Augusto Boal and Elizabeth
LeCompte, concluding that 'one might start to invent computers as
performance' (McKenzie 1994: 90). Around the same time, Sue-Ellen
Case pointed out that the performativity of human–computer interaction was even visible in the prosthetic use of the mouse in that
'[t]ogether, the mouse and the human constitute an entity' (Case
1996: 94). She also suggested that the process of writing on a computer
screen is in itself performative (Case 1995: 333) and predicted that 'if

the computer screen is soon to become *the* screen to the world as well as for our own so-called private production, its space will be *the* contested arena of the symbolic organization of cultural and economic power' (*ibid*.: 334, original emphases). Later, Steve Dixon showed that the small digital screen intrinsically produces Brechtian alienation and hence 'encourages users to view the material from a more objective perspective' (Dixon 1999: 141). In fact, '[j]ust as the stuttering jerks and poor resolution of CCTV footage gives gritty realism and sense of "truth" to views of street and shops, so too does the computer's flickering QuickTime proscenium' (*ibid*.). In other words, the very way in which the screen operates encourages the viewer to interpret the world of the screen as truth, as presenting something which is or was 'really there'. But what appears on the screen is not necessarily an objective recording of an outer reality. It might not even be somebody's reconstruction of a real event. What is important about these reflections is that they point to the most intriguing characteristic of the computer screen: the fact that it is through the screen that the viewer is increasingly experiencing the world, and yet the viewer is still reading the screen as if it were presenting an *objective* view of the world, as if it were a prosthetic of the viewer's own senses.

Virtual reality has been defined as referring 'to technologies or environments that provide realistic cues to some or all the senses, sufficient to engender in the participant a willing suspension of disbelief' (Tice and Jacobson in Jacobson 1992: 280). It can be delivered in three forms:

- In an 'immersive' or 'inclusive' way (through goggles, gloves or datasuits) in which 'the participant feels as if he or she is inside the graphic, or virtual world' (*ibid*.: 281).
- Through a 'desktop VR', which involves viewing the 3D world through a window or a screen. Here the 'participant steers through the virtual world using physical controls provided by special 3D data input services' (*ibid*.).
- Through what has been described as 'third-person VR', in which 'you view and steer an image of yourself interacting in the virtual world' (*ibid*.).

All three delivery forms refer to three-dimensional visual worlds in which a viewer can interact with the environment and the people or objects this may contain as if 'he or she were inside the image' (Robins 1996: 44). As David Z. Saltz points out, '[v]irtual reality systems fully immerse a subject in a computer-simulated environment, a purely virtual space with no physical, real-world spatial co-ordinates. Telepresence, by contrast, uses computers, telecommunications and robotics to conjoin two or more real-world locations' (Saltz 2001: 70). Although, as Saltz points out, there is a substantial difference between virtual reality and telepresence, both create a virtual environment which, in the case of virtual reality, is totally simulated; and, in the case of telepresence, is the remediatised merging of two real locations. In neither case is the environment *actually* there.

This book is about virtual reality environments and about environments created through telepresence. It is also about other, diverse environments which nevertheless in many ways share theatricality, performativity and, last but not least, of course, some degree of virtuality. The first type of environment analysed is that created by HTML or VRML. Here, the viewer is likely to navigate complex textual environments and literally *enter* the work of art. The second type is that created by cyborg performance, which, like hypertext, disperses the viewer and is often able to present the world, whether that inside or outside the performer's body, as inside out. In revisiting notions of the human through conceptual and practical experimentations with the cyborg, it has proved essential to redefine the concept and practice of nature by investigating it per se, while also recreating it artificially. Thus, the third section of this book focuses on how artists' attempts to recreate nature, through artificial reality or via genetic manipulation, can be read as a form of theatre of the real. Finally, the last type of environment presented in this book is that created by the hypersurface, the surface which brings together materiality and simulation and thereby constitutes the perfect viewing space of the real. In fact, there is a wide variety of possibilities for both interpreting and making virtual theatre that go well beyond any canonical interpretation of both theatre and computer science. Since theatre is the place to view, to observe the real, a virtual theatre is a place in which the real, which of course includes the viewer, is remediatised, experienced twice, as the viewer is both in the real world and remediatised by the mechanical apparatus of the virtual theatre. In other words, a virtual theatre is one which through virtuality is able not only to include the viewer within the work of art but also to distribute their presence 'globally' in both the real and the simulated information world.

All the virtual theatre forms analysed in this book share the capacity to multiply and disperse the viewer's point of view, thus creating the simulation of a condition that the viewer also experiences in the real, since 'we no longer exist as playwrights or actors but as terminals of multiple networks' (Baudrillard 1988: 16). However, virtual theatre does not only disperse the viewer inside the work of art, but allows them to be 'both *in* the picture and [have] *control* over it' (Morse 1998: 182, original emphases). And although what the viewer experiences in virtual theatre is mainly the product of a simulation, the effects of that simulation over the viewer are very real. In other words, the fact that the real is seen and experienced as simulation does not make it less real in terms of its effect over the viewer. Moreover, virtual theatre totally subverts canonical uses of time and space in art in that '[w]ith the interfacing of computer terminals and video monitors, distinctions of *here* and *there* no longer mean anything' (Virilio 1991: 13, original emphases). Thus the very existence of virtual theatre challenges notions of locality and regionality as well as globality, and even renders the idea of art being *in* and *about* a location somewhat redundant. In fact, as suggested by Peter Weibel,

> [m]edia like cinema, video and, later, computer are about dislocation, while classical art is about location. Theater takes place in time and space on a stage; a sculpture is bound in space, as is architecture. But from the telegraph in the 1840s onwards it became possible to separate message from messenger [. . .] The new aesthetics is about dislocation; the message goes from one locus to another.
>
> (in Mulder and Post 2000: 59)

Interestingly, virtual theatre both takes place within a real location and, because of the remediatisation, produces dislocation. But not only does the artwork exist in multiple locations, the viewer too is able to become translocal in that they too are part of the work of art. Just as the viewer is no longer entirely in one location, they are also no longer viewing something that has a clear beginning, middle and end. As in Gilles Deleuze and Félix Guattari's rhizome, which has no beginning or end, only a middle (Deleuze and Guattari 1988: 25), the virtual reality viewer is always entering something that has a past and a future which span well beyond them. Virtual theatre, like the reality it allows us to view, is made of fragments, segments of information. In Deleuze and Guattari's view, life is 'spatially and socially segmented' (*ibid*.: 208). Virtual theatre too reflects and exposes this signification.

Virtual theatre constructs itself through the interaction between the viewer and the work of art which allows the viewer to be present in both the real and the virtual environment. This interaction is perhaps the most important characteristic of virtual theatre. Popper identifies 'active participation' as originating in the works of artists such as

Yacov Agam, Jesus Raphael Soto, Tinguely and Pol Bury during the 1950s, which introduced a 'third dimension', giving a choice to the spectators to intervene in the creative process (Popper 1993: 26). A variety of artists subsequently explored interactivity, including Jeffrey Shaw, Roy Ascott, Myron Krueger, Jean-Louis Boissier, Stephen Wilson and Edmond Couchot. Through interaction with the work, the viewer/performer is often able to modify the work, occasionally even to disperse their viewpoint within the work, by flattening themself into the work of the image or becoming an avatar. Thus, in many ways, virtual reality, and so, to some extent, virtual theatre, becomes 'the place where the subject sees itself as "out of joint" [. . .] The user finds him/herself in a specific inter-subjective relation with his/her double [. . .] this double is a kind of exteriorization, a kind of spectral creature' (Marina Gržinić in Weibel and Druckrey 2001: 77). This double becomes the viewer's closest claim to a verification of their own being. This is because, as suggested by Baudrillard, '[s]ince it is no longer possible to base any claim on one's own existence, there is nothing for it but to perform an *appearing act* without concerning oneself with *being* – or even with *being seen*. So it is not: I exist, I am here! But rather: I am visible, I am an image – look! look!' (Baudrillard 1993: 23, original emphases).

Through virtual theatre, the societies of information and of flesh and blood are temporarily merged. Here, as in Guy Debord's society of spectacle, our life no longer belongs to ourselves but to the 'spectacle', the theatre of the real, and it is through the experience of that theatre that the viewer is able to reconstruct themself in the real. In interpreting this form of theatre, however, we have to remember McLuhan's assertion that we can look at the present only through the spectacles of the preceding age (McLuhan 1987: 243). Like Walter Benjamin's 'Angel of History', we are blown into the future but all we can see is the detritus of the past. Virtual theatre, the spectacle of the real, is, of course, our future, but what we see inside it is still nothing but our past. This is why, rather than its appearance, all we can focus on is its act of disappearance.

1

HYPERTEXTUALITIES

Hypertextualities are forms of textualities that are rendered through HTML, an abbreviation of hypertext mark-up language. Whether textual or intermedial, hypertextualities are fluid and open forms that allow the reader or viewer to move beyond the world of the interface and penetrate the realm of the work of art. Hypertextualities are fluid in that they dissolve the separation of the roles of subject (viewer) and object (work of art). They are similarly open, because they allow the viewer to move towards completion of the work of art while also permitting future viewers to continue to expand and enrich it. Hypertextualities introduce a performative dimension to the acts of reading and viewing. In order to be engaged with, hypertexts need to be acted upon, and reading hypertext becomes equivalent to putting it into action. By bringing the viewer into the work of art, and allowing them to exist in both the real and the virtual, hypertextualities also multiply the viewer's position. So hypertextualities are complex and sophisticated textualities that expand the world of text into the world of action.

The performance of hypertext: theory and practice

Although the concept of hypertext was anticipated as early as 1945 by Vannever Bush's essay 'As We May Think', the term itself was coined only in 1965 by Ted Nelson indicating 'non-sequential writing with reader-controlled links' (Nelson in Delany and Landow 1992: 106). Subsequently, George Landow defined hypertext as 'text composed of blocks of words (or images) linked electronically by multiple paths, chains or trails in an open-ended, perpetually unfinished textuality described by the terms *link*, *node*, *network*, *web*, and *path*' (Landow 1997: 3, original emphases). As pointed out by

Landow's definition, hypertext has come to indicate a form of writing in which specific sections of a given text are linked in a non-linear way. In hypertext, the reader controls these links, so hypertext therefore represents the embodiment of the poststructuralist concept of text (Aarseth 1997: 58). Instead of plot, hypertext produces 'activities effectuated but not controlled by the user' (*ibid*.: 112).

Hypertext induces actions within space: to read a hypertext entails reading the text as well as the space within which the hypertext is encoded. In this sense, hypertext is each text forming the hypertextual structure, but also the path of interrelatedness connecting each segment to other segments. To read both text and code, the reader has to enter, so to speak, the space of hypertext and engage in a series of activities: so '[e]lectronic writing is both a visual and a verbal description. It is not the writing of a place, but rather a writing *with* places, spatially realized topics' (Bolter 1991: 25, original emphasis). In hypertext writing, words thus constitute 'portals' (Novak 1995: 46), and hypertext structures can be seen as virtual architectures in which words function as doors, gateways to other doors. Pierre Lévy shows that 'hypertexts are organised following a fractal logic in that each link may be a further link' (Lévy 1999: 32). Thus, reading a hypertext not only implies actively moving through space to find contents and to explore the space containing the contents, but also to observe the structural and formal patterns characterising each fractal section and to study their potential interrelatedness to the fleeting whole. In this sense, hypertextual readers negotiate the symbolic and the real levels at once: like any other form of art, hypertext is a discourse on both form and content, medium and message.

Arguably, a number of classics can be read as hypertext, such as James Joyce's *Ulysses* (1922), which cannot be understood without a map of Dublin. The Talmud also can be seen as a hypertext. The same is true for Jorge Luis Borges's *The Garden of Forking Paths* (1941), which is written as a labyrinth in such a way that various futures are represented simultaneously. The novel sees the narrator, Dr Yu Tsun, a German spy during the First World War, murdering one Steven Albert, who had devoted his life to the study of a novel called *The Garden of Forking Paths*, written by Ts'ui Pên, an ancestor of the narrator. Similar puns on the relationship between present and multiple futures are explored in films such as Harold Ramis's *Groundhog Day* (1993) and Akira Kurosawa's classic *Rashomon* (1950), in which the same crime is narrated by four different people. This is also true for Italo Calvino's *If on a Winter's Night a Traveller* (1979), which is a long meditation on fiction-making that keeps unravelling and restarting. Yet, although books have always behaved, to some extent, hypertextually, a hypertextual network can extend indefinitely, whereas a printed text cannot (Bolter in Delany and Landow 1992: 111). The difference between text and hypertext lies precisely in the role played by the medium itself, HTML, but also its host, the Net, allowing the reader a far more interactive role that includes the possibility of entering the work of art by the means of the very act of reading itself.

Landow describes hypertext as 'text composed of blocks of text – what Roland Barthes terms lexia – and the electronic links that join them' (Landow 1997: 3). The concept of hypermedia extends the notion of hypertext by including images (photos, films, graphics, etc.) and sound. To explain hypertext further, Landow uses Mikhail Bakhtin's idea of the dialogic and the polyphonic novel (*ibid.*: 36). He argues that hypertext is composed of bodies of linked texts that have no primary axis of organisation: they have no centre (*ibid.*: 36–7). Interestingly, he describes Gilles Deleuze and Félix Guattari's masterpiece *A Thousand Plateaus* (1980) as a 'proto-hypertext' (*ibid.*: 38). Like the rhizome, hypertext has 'multiple entryways and exits' and connects 'any point to any other point' (*ibid.*: 40). Most importantly, in hypertext the functions of the reader and the writer become intertwined and it is the reader, not the author, who determines how reading proceeds (*ibid.*: 282). Intermedia, like all hypertext systems, permits the individual user to choose their own 'center of investigation and experience' (Landow 1989: 185).

To explain hypertext through a metaphor, Silvio Gaggi quotes Jorge Luis Borges's story *The Library of Babel* (1941; Gaggi 1997: 100–1), in which Borges imagines a library that is an infinite network of hexagonal galleries containing all possible books:

> the minutely detailed history of the future, the archangels' autobiographies, the faithful catalogue of the Library, thousands and thousands of false catalogues, the demonstration of the fallacy of those catalogues, the demonstration of the fallacy of the true catalogue, the Gnostic gospel of Basilides, the commentary on that gospel, the commentary on the commentary on that gospel, the true story of your death, the translation of every book in all languages, the interpolations of every book in all books.
>
> (Borges 1964: 54)

As Gaggi shows, Babel's library has no centre, and every position in the library could act as a provisional centre (Gaggi 1997: 101).

Hypertext, just like Babel's library, has no beginning, middle or end. Its architecture mirrors the infinite nature of the universe. Yet in hypertext not only is the reader the explorer, and hence the true author of the work of art, but also their presence is written into the work of art. The reader is therefore inside the meta-architecture, inside the work of art, and it is through the reader's 'interaction' with the text that the work of art manifests itself.

It was George Landow who first pointed out the parallels between computer hypertext and critical theory (Landow 1997: 2) and showed that the pre-history of hypertext stemmed from critical theory. He pointed out that in *S/Z* (1970) Roland Barthes describes a textual form that is very similar to hypertext, just as Michel Foucault in *The Archaeology of Knowledge* (1969) conceives of text in terms of network and links (*ibid.*: 3). Likewise, Jacques Derrida's *Glas* (1974) is organised 'hypertextually', the links here being represented by different fonts, sizes and sections on the page. Although Landow shows that the very concept of hypertext is not new, it is only through an electronic form that hypertext can actually manifest itself. The inheritance of critical theory does, however, show how, upon entering a hypertext, the hypertextual reader effectively enters a text that is always already metatextual. No hypertext therefore exists in isolation – Net reading is an acting out of hypertextualities.

As Landow points out, although hypertextual practice simulates spatiality, the reader experiences it differently, as the goal is always reachable: 'whereas navigation presupposes that one finds oneself at the centre of a spatial world in which desired items lie at varying distances from one's own location, hypertext presupposes an experiential world in which the goal is always potentially but one jump or link away' (in Delany and Landow 1992: 102). A hypertext structure forms a network of nodes and links that happen in virtual space and real time and that simulate real travel but in which the distance covered is always determined by the passing of time and not by real movement in space. In this sense, hypertext allows for the possibility of a journey that must always arrive at the viewer/performer's physical point of departure.

One 'experiences a hypertext as a changeable montage' (Landow in Lunenfeld 2001: 170), and structures that help us visualise what is behind the screen include a network, a tree diagram, a web or a nest of Chinese boxes (Delany and Landow 1992: 4). In fact, most hypertextual browsers and symbols imply the notion of travel – Internet Explorer; Netscape; Net; anchor; surfing the Net, and so on – so it is therefore unsurprising that the discourses about the writing and reading of hypertext are mainly about orientation, and that surfing the Net implies the maintenance of a certain equilibrium and the capacity of finding one's way back home. Thus, hypertext is a virtual *Odyssey* in which the points of departure and arrival coincide.

In the world of virtual reality, where everything is text and text is action, the rules of the space/time continuum are subverted, as is shown by Paul Virilio: 'we are seeing the beginnings of a *"generalized arrival"* whereby everything arrives without having to leave, the nineteenth-century elimination of the journey (that is, of the space interval and of time) combining with the abolition of *departure* at the end of the twentieth, the journey thereby losing its successive components and being overtaken by *arrival* alone' (Virilio 1997: 16, original emphases). Through virtual reality, inertia has come to represent the defining condition of modernity (Virilio 2000). Telecommunication has replaced real action and an instantaneous present has substituted travel in time and space so that everything happens without us needing to go anywhere. To explain this metaphor, Virilio offers the example of a swimming pool in Tokyo where people train against a tide such that 'you have to exert the power of movement to remain where you are' and 'whoever exercises here, then, becomes less a moving body than an island, a *pole of inertia*' (*ibid.*: 17, original emphasis). As in Virilio's pool, in virtual reality '*everything arrives without any need to depart*' (*ibid.*: 20, original emphasis). Hypertextual travel, just like the experience of virtual reality, is travel with no *real* movement, but the actual condition of hypertext is that of a permanent state of arrival.

One of the earliest and most complex hypertexts is Stuart Moulthrop's hypertextual novel *Victory Garden* (1991), whose title echoes that of the Borges story and which is also in the shape of a labyrinth. *Victory Garden* contains 993 textual segments connected by 2,804 links. A map of its overall structure is offered so that the reader can determine from where to enter the piece and also how to move from one section to another. The story follows a number of characters during the first Gulf War but is set in a university in the southern United States in 1991. The reader may follow people home or to their workplace, listen to the official coverage of the first Gulf War (via CNN transcripts) or read the protagonist's letters. The text functions like 'a maze' and the war is represented as a 'hyperreal event' (Gaggi 1997: 130 and 127). Yet, at the centre of the piece is the death of Emily Runebird, an army reserve soldier and student of cultural anthropology killed in her barracks by an enemy missile. The attack is represented by shattered text: 'her passing is represented – or *not* represented (death being at least one possibility of the real that stands outside of any representation of it) – by an image that simulates a crack in the reader's monitor. When the reader hits the return button, the next screen is entirely black' (*ibid.*: 127, original emphasis). Death, here, invades the monitor and thus penetrates the interface, not only affecting the reader's understanding of the text itself but also obscuring the medium, subtracting the interface from the viewer.

Moulthrop followed up *Victory Garden* with *Dreamtime* (1992). The latter piece is less linear than the former and contains more visual components, such as drawings and icons, and sounds. Some of the lexias look like email messages containing the date and the time when the reader looks at the text, hence 'confusing reality and representation' (Gaggi 1997: 135). The lexias are small segments of dreams by a number of dreamers. There is no privileged axis of movement (*ibid.*: 135). Here, again, representation penetrates reality via the interface, thereby including the reader's textual actions into the work of art.

Michael Joyce's *afternoon, a story* (1987) is an interactive narrative presented through different versions of a story. In one version the reader follows the narrator's quest to find his ex-wife and son, while in another they may follow the history and thoughts of his analyst and friend. While in one version an accident seems to have occurred, in another no accident has happened (Douglas 1993: 22). The piece comprises 539 textual segments with 951 links. The reader can hit the return key, the equivalent of turning the page (Gaggi 1997: 123), click on certain words on the screen or click the Browse icon and then choose from the available options. The exploration of the text is akin to the exploration of a vast house or castle (Bolter 1991: 125). Occasionally, the reader's response to a 'yes or no' question directs them to a specific part of the story. But sometimes the characters' background merges clearly and sometimes it is disjointed and confusing (Gaggi 1997: 123). Bolter suggests that *afternoon, a story* shows that 'there is no story at all; there are only readings. Or if we say that the story of "Afternoon" is the sum of all its readings, then we must understand the story as a structure that can embrace contradictory outcomes' (Bolter 1991: 124). Like most hypertexts, *afternoon, a story* is also metatextual and therefore a direct challenge to the act of reading itself: '"Afternoon" is about the problem of its own reading' (*ibid.*: 127).

Since these early examples of hypertext writing, hypertext fiction and theory have been explored in numerous directions. Charles Deemer's hyperdramas comprise original pieces incorporating re-writes of classic play texts, including Anton Chekhov's *The Seagull* (1895), in which Deemer wrote scenes for the off-stage characters.

Meanwhile, Sharon Denning's *Exquisite Corpse* (2000) 'is a database of possible stories, a map of tellings and retellings, a network of routes from one beginning to many possible endings' (Denning in Leopoldseder and Schöpf 2000: 32). In *Exquisite Corpse* each chapter can branch into an infinite number of stories and users can choose to read existing branches or add their own. Both classical and more contemporary examples of hypertext show not only that it is often both meta- and intertextual but also that the reader, in their role as interactive operator, is far more active than when interpreting conventional text, and thereby, literally, enters the architecture of hypertext, becoming themself another hypertextuality within the World Wide Web.

Brenda Laurel has shown that the potential of computers lies not so much in their capacity to perform calculations as in their ability to '*represent action in which humans could participate*' (Laurel 1993: 1, original emphasis). In this context, the interface 'becomes the arena for the performance of some task in which both human and computer have a role' (*ibid.*: 7). As hypertextual experimentation develops further, it is becoming clear that, in hypertext, text is action and that the interface is the very space of the interchange, the space of the action. It follows that not only is hypertext a new performative medium that combines elements of film, video and theatre, yet supersedes all three by including the viewer in the work of art, but also that in it the viewer is able to combine the performance of both text and metatext – narrative and critical theory. And since one of the characteristics of hypertextual fiction is the absence of a clearly identifiable ending (Douglas 1993: 28), hypertext also subverts narrative and dramaturgical theory by always ensuring that the true 'ending' of the work of art is outside the work of art itself and resides within the world of the viewer. In hypertext, narratives never end and viewers, themselves transformed into HTML, become just another hypertextuality waiting to be read by someone else.

Simulating catastrophe: the case of Jodi and 01001011101011101.ORG

The art form that has most daringly and originally explored the human–computer interface is Net Art. The term Net Art was coined by a user in an email to Vuk Cosic in 1995 (Weibel and Druckrey 2001: 25) and was subsequently used at a conference in Trieste in 1996 (Baumgärtel in Weibel and Druckrey 2001: 158) to define those art practices that take place on and through the Net. An early example of Net Art is Douglas Davis's *The World's Longest Sentence* (1994), which is based on a program that prevents spectators/writers from using full stops so that they become 'part of an ongoing statement that will never end' (Baumgärtel 2001: 62). Davis's *MetaBody* (1997) follows the same collective principle, except that the users are asked to contribute pictures of the human body to the site (*ibid.*: 62–4). Likewise, in Roy Ascott's *La Plissure du texte: A Planetary Fairy Tale* (1983), one of the pioneering examples of Net Art, various artists connected through the Net wrote a text to which the audience could also contribute. In contrast, in a more recent piece by David Link, *Poetry Machine (version 1.0)* (2001), the viewer entered an environment in which they could watch a screen filling with text read out by a single male voice. Here the text is either, almost cannibalistically, derived from the Net or written by previous or current viewers by typing on to a suspended keyboard.

Just as these Net artists all variously engaged with the possibility of metasentences and metatexts, others saw the potential for experimentation with the interface itself. Programs were thus developed whose aim it was to disturb the interface and thereby challenge not only the relationship between the viewer and the work of art, but also the very assumptions around the location of Net Art. Thus Antoni Abad, for instance, created *Z* (1999), which consists of a fly that is able to rub its front legs, walk and fly across the screen (Weibel and Druckrey 2001: 178). Likewise, but to a more disruptive effect, Cosic wrote HTML documents that crash the browser (Baumgärtel in Weibel and Druckrey 2001: 159). Both pieces more or less ironically challenge the assumption that Net Art is located, so to speak, *inside* the Net, by interfering with the actual interface and thereby forcing the viewer into an action that is no longer aimed at the reading or even the creation of a text, or a metatext, but rather towards the defensive act of liberating oneself from the 'invasive' virus-like program. As shown by Tilman Baumgärtel, '[t]he established net protocol, such as, for example, HTML, the code with which WebPages are "written", is expressively thematized and questioned by some of the most interesting net art projects' (*ibid.*). Such projects challenge the viewers to question the very dynamics by which they receive the work of art, and often draw their attention to the complexity of the Internet as a medium in its own right.

The company which perhaps most famously engages with the interface and the complex relationship of viewer and Net Art consists of the Dutch-Belgian artists Joan Heemskerk and Dirk Paesmans, who, since 1995, have operated under the name Jodi. Heemskerk and

Paesmans work primarily by manipulating HTML code so that the viewer is no longer able to distinguish between code and art. In Jodi's work 'the creative coding – hypertext markup language (HTML), virtual reality markup language (VRML), and whatever comes next – is visible at the same moment as the audiovisual object' (Lunenfeld 2000: 83). Not only does the code (the medium) become the message, but the viewer is given no indication of how to travel through the interface and interpret the code which constitutes the work of art.

Jodi's site, Jodi.org (1997), has been described as follows:

> [t]he first screen is simple: lines of green characters on a black screen, with a green highlighting function cycling down. [. . .] There are no identifiers, no marks of authorship or ownership, no indication that clicking on this essentially meaningless screen will lead into the rest of the site. The next screen to appear creates a vaguely three-dimensional, grid-dled space with variously coloured directional arrows. Clicking on any element of this page simply reshuffles the arrangement and direction of the arrows. This section is indeed interactive but to absolutely no purpose.
>
> (Lunenfeld 2000: 82)

In Jodi.org, not only does the code become the work of art, the 'inside' or medium transforming into the 'outside' or message, but the text becomes metatextual. As a labyrinth, however, the site leads nowhere: all the paths are only pretending to take the unaware viewer to other paths, trapping them within the work of art and leaving them with no other choice but that of trying to escape the work altogether.

Jodi's subsequent work, viewable on CD-ROM, *OSS/****** (1998), challenges the interface further by making the very desktop shake, sink and flicker:

> [i]f you click the mouse hoping to get rid of this computer virus or whatever it is, windows open up everywhere, your cursor starts leaving a trail, your pull-down menus become either empty or unintelligible, thick horizontal stripes start running across your screen, suddenly changing into vertical ones. There is no escape. And in the unlikely event that you do escape, your pointer becomes invisible and you must click on one of the many plus signs of the screen in order to get away.
>
> (Mulder and Post 2000: 99)

It is quite clear from *OSS/***** that Jodi wants the viewer to have a physical experience of the computer (Mulder and Post 2000: 100). 'This is the end of the pretty pictures. Your operating system has just started to attack you'*(ibid.)*. The catastrophe of *OSS/***** is that there is no decipherable metatext, just as there is no longer a comfortable work of art to view. The only action 'happening' in this piece, apart from the running of the actual program, is the viewer's attempt to stop the crash; in other words, the viewer's attempt to prevent the work of art from happening at all. As Baumgärtel notes '[t]he browser suddenly takes on a life of its own and, by itself, opens more and more new little windows dancing wildly across the monitor and seems somehow to be playing catch-as-catch-can with the user's mouse and cursor' (Baumgärtel 2001: 166). Mesmerised by the flickering screen, images changing size, moving from left to right and vice versa, grids appearing and disappearing, unanticipated piercing noises, incomplete table menus that contain nothing, and numbers containing other numbers, the viewer must feel like they are drowning in an HTML code over which they have no control and no understanding. Here 'everything is just the opposite of what "normally" happens on a desktop. If you don't press the mouse, you draw a line on this surface; if you click, you hear a sound instead of activating an icon; the drop down menus have no text, while the windows are full of text gibberish' *(ibid.*: 170). In *OSS/*****, Jodi thus subverts the dynamics by which viewers habitually engage with the interface not only by presenting the interface itself as the subject (Paesmans in Baumgärtel 2001: 170), but also by creating the situation by which the viewer, rather than navigating the work of art, loses themself in it and, rather than trying to derive significance from it, has to surrender to the simulated catastrophe they are forced to witness. By creating works that are acts of provocation, Jodi seems to be alerting its audience to the fact that the Net, with all its texts and hypertexts, is not in itself 'transparent', and that it is often what is encoded *behind* the visible text that affects the readers and their understanding of what is narrated by and through the Web.

In September 1999, a clone of Jodi's website appeared on the Web. The site contained no modifications of the original and was mistaken by many for it. The new site was written by the anonymous Italian group 0100101110101101.ORG, who have variously been described as 'cultural terrorists' and 'media dandies' (0100101110101101.ORG 2002). With Jodi's clone, 0100101110101101.ORG wanted to demonstrate that 'certain ideas and practices – such as the authenticity and uniqueness of an artwork – must be considered obstacles to the

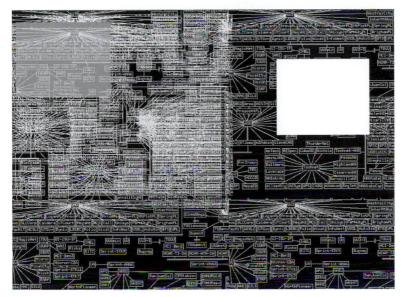

Figure 1 %20Transfer, 0100101110101101.ORG, 1999, no copyright. Screen shot from 0100101110101101.ORG's copy of the website Jodi.org.

development of Web art' (*ibid.*). By operating anonymously as hack-activists, 0100101110101101.ORG aims to destabilise the Web as a 'safe' environment and expose capitalistic and global control methods operating in both the real and the virtual.

In this context, 0100101110101101.ORG developed a number of clone sites, such as vaticano.org (1998), in which it created and main-tained for a year a clone of the official Vatican site; hell.com (1999), in which a copy was made of the leading Net art museum; and *Ftpermutations* (2001), where the directory naming twelve artists participating in the Korea Web Art Festival was substituted with another site (0100101110101101.ORG 2002). 0100101110101101. ORG also created Web Art viruses such as in biennale.py (2001), where, in response to an invitation to participate in the forty-ninth Biennale in Venice, the company created a computer virus which was spread from the Slovene Pavilion on the opening day of the exhibition (*ibid.*). Finally, the company has been exposing the vulner-ability of the mechanisms we adopt for the protection of individual privacy. Thus, for instance, *Vopos* (2002) allows for the constant virtual monitoring of the location of two members of the group via telephone, satellite and the Internet and the earlier piece *life_sharing* (2001), through which the group shares its files on the Web,

Date: Sun, 17 Sep 2000 21:00:01 +0900
From: Marc Voge marc@totalmuseum.org
Organization: Total Museum
To: jodi@0100101110101101.ORG, jodi@jodi.org
Subject: Project 8, Seoul

Dear jodi,

   Hi, I'm Marc Voge, and I'm the guest curator at the Total Museum
of Contemporary Art in Seoul, South Korea. I would like to invite
you to participate in Project 8, a prestigious international show
that features eight Web artists this year.
   In the recent past this annual group exhibition has invited such
well-known artists as Tony Cragg, Thomas Ruff, Toni Grand and Andy
Goldsworthy. The Total Museum is also proud to include in this year's
Web Project 8 the SFMOMA Webby Award-winning Korean artist Young-hae
Chang.
   The show is scheduled to open on December 1, 2000, and each Web
artist's honorarium will be $1000 U.S. For this sum, we invite you
to create an original piece that can be E-mailed to the Total Museum
site by mid-November. We realize that the two months between now and
then is a relatively short period. Our hope is that we can inspire
Web artists to undertake short-term projects with original results.
   We also plan to create a CD-ROM of the exhibition.
   I hope you will participate. Please feel free to E-mail me any
questions you might have at marc@totalmuseum.org.
   I look forward to hearing from you soon.

Yours truly,

Marc Voge

http://www.totalmuseum.org

Date: Tue, 19 Sep 2000 02:19:00 +0200
From: jodi@0100101110101101.ORG
To: marc@totalmuseum.org
BCC: jodi@jodi.org
Subject: Re: Project 8, Seoul

Marc Voge wrote:

> we invite you to
> create an original piece that can be E-mailed to the Total Museum
> site by mid-November. We realize that the two months between now
> and then is a relatively short period.

Attachment: 401 Authorization Required

Date: Wed, 20 Sep 2000 13:22:39 +0900
From: Marc Voge marc@totalmuseum.org
Organization: Total Museum
To: jodi@0100101110101101.ORG
Subject: Re: Project 8, Seoul

Dear jodi@0100101110101101.ORG,

   Thanks for the piece! It's great! I love it!
   There's only one problem. I realize now that I've made a terrible
mistake -- that you're not jodi, you're jodi@0100101110101101.ORG.
You see, I just received an E-mail from jodi who says you're a "fake."
 According to jodi, you're a group of Italian artists in Bologna
(a city that I love, by the way) pretending to be jodi.
   It's really too bad, because your work is original -- and quite
different from jodi's work.
   Why are you pretending to be jodi? Why not just be yourselves?

Yours,

Marc Voge

Figure 2 Email exchange between curator Marc Voge and
0100101110101101.ORG, 0100101110101101.ORG, 2000, no
copyright.

'radically challenges the concept of privacy and explores the contradictions of intellectual property' (*ibid.*).

This interplay of clones, and the subsequent discourse about control, was even further exposed when, on 24 December 1999, Amy Alexander opened a site called plagiarist.org in which she introduced a clone of www.0100101110101101.org (and hence also a clone of their clone). 0100101110101101.ORG responded by linking its site to the one created by Alexander (Dreher 2002). Described, in Baudrillardian fashion, as a copy without an original (Weibel in Dreher 2002) or, better, as a set of copies with no originals, this endless mirroring of clones of other clones by companies that use the Web as their stage leaves the viewer wondering what it is they are actually witnessing. Unable to distinguish between the medium and its content or message, unable even to distinguish between the 'original' site and its clones, the viewer becomes painfully aware that the performance of Web Art and the subsequent interaction between the author/artists and the viewer are far more complex than the simple access to a computer and the Web. By means of simulation and interference, both Jodi and 0100101110101101.ORG take the viewer through provocative and dizzying levels of complex HTML, which demonstrate how profoundly the virtual can impact on our perception of the real. Not only have these companies variously exposed the complexity of what appears to be simple text, HTML, but they have shown the aesthetic and political impact that the modification or monitoring and control of HTML can imply – the real catastrophe of HTML being the disempowerment to which the viewers inevitably expose themselves when entering the corporate world of the World Wide Web.

Spatialising the interface: Jeffrey Shaw and Masaki Fujihata's metatexts

The exploration of the interface is not confined to Net Art. In fact, since the 1960s, a number of alternative artists have been experimenting with the interface and interactivity by exploring their potentials, primarily aesthetically, but also, on occasion, politically. Early interactive art thus appeared in Fluxus, Environmental Art, Happenings and in works by artists such as John Cage, Merce Cunningham and Robert Rauschenberg. The last of these developed *Soundings* (1968), an early interactive environment in which the audience could illuminate a number of panels by speaking into a set of microphones (Kostelanetz 1994: 132). Already at that time Rauschenberg was interested in developing environments in which temperature, smell and sound could be influenced by the viewer (Dinkla 1997: 36). Indeed, throughout the 1960s one of the most influential post-war theatre companies, the Living Theatre, was using some degree of interactivity to draw attention to the aesthetic and political content of its work, and to ensure, in post-Brechtian fashion, that the audience would become aware of its political implications.

However, the artist who is often credited with the development of one of the first interactive mediatised works, *Participation TV I* (1966), is Nam June Paik. *Participation TV I*, whose principal elements Paik had exhibited as early as 1963, consisted of a magnet located on a television set which transformed its electronic image in response to the viewer's voice. Similarly, his *Video Synthesizer* (1969–70), created in collaboration with Shuya Abe, allowed for the alteration of video recordings and the creation of synthetic visual forms. Though early examples of interactive art, Paik's experiments functioned by dislodging a given mediatised image through a synthetic process, hence altering, deteriorating or amplifying the real by means of the actual medium. Already in Paik's early work the viewer is responsible for the work of art and determines its duration, as well as its structure and exact direction. These pieces reveal a major characteristic of all interactive works: namely, their capacity to 'respond' to the viewer (Hünnekens 1997: 19). Here, the interactivity is not merely an added characteristic; it provides the 'content' and 'message', and it is within this interactivity, within the encounter between the viewer, the object and the medium, that the work of art takes place.

Closed-circuit installations from the 1960s in which the viewer is confronted with their own image pioneered another fundamental characteristic of interactive art (Hünnekens 1997: 22). In works such as Bruce Nauman's *Live/Taped Video Corridor* (1968–9), the viewers were confronted, on one or more monitors, with their own images recorded from an earlier moment in time, so prompting a realisation of having been 'caught' by the medium and affecting the displacement of time/space at the heart of the work of art. The video helps the viewer 'to see' through 'the jungle of the real' (*ibid.*: 23) by acting as a destabilising factor and thereby relocating the viewer in a universe in which they are simultaneously viewer and viewed. The viewer's sudden 'recognition' (*ibid.*: 25) and the subsequent displacement, or even *Unheimlichkeit*, produced by the act of seeing oneself simultaneously from different perspectives, real and virtual, are here the result of the interaction which returns nothing but the uncomfortable and yet ironic awareness that we are always part of the world we watch.

So interactivity has been a major theme in experimental art since the 1960s, but it has only been since the beginning of the 1990s that the term 'interactive art' has come into common usage, demarking a wide range of experimentation in different media. Popper describes interactive art as presenting 'a flow of data (images, text, sound) and an array of cybernetic, adaptive and (one might say) *intelligent* structures, environments and networks (as performances, events, personal encounters and private experiences) in such a way that the observer can affect the flow, alter the structure, interact with the environment or navigate the network, thus becoming directly involved in acts of transformation and creation' (Popper 1993: 172, original emphasis). It is precisely this 'intelligent' capacity of allowing the viewer to transform and create that represents the fundamental characteristic of interactive art, a form which is therefore defined by the fact that it is both closed in its finality of aesthetic interactivity and open in its capacity of being constantly subverted by the viewer.

In interactive art not only is the viewer responsible for the realisation of the work of art, but they activate the parameters by which the work of art manifests itself through both real and virtual realms in what is therefore both a 'representation [and] a construction of reality' (Ascott in Hünnekens 1997: 68). Not only is interactivity an 'extension of the structure of the work of art' (Shaw in Hünnekens 1997: 46), but it is, by implication, an extension of the viewer, a widening of the space in which the real and the virtual are allowed, however paradoxically, to co-exist. In the encounter with the interactive art object, the viewer therefore experiences the realisation that they can be both viewer and viewed, inside and outside the work of art, existing both virtually and in the real. In interactive art, the difference between the viewer/observer, the environment and the world dissipates (Weibel in Hünnekens 1997: 83).

By not only redefining the relationship of viewer and viewed but reinventing the dynamics of the very environment in which the encounter between the viewer and viewed takes place, Jeffrey Shaw argues that '[a] new aesthetics comes to the fore. The art-work is more and more embodied in the interface, in the articulation of a space where the art-work as an artefact seems to disappear altogether and only communication between the viewers remains' (Shaw in Duguet, Klotz and Weibel 1997: 157). In this way interactive art is not merely constituted by the object or the viewer, but by the encounter between the two. Interactive art is therefore first of all an *environment*, and all that is contained within it at any one moment in time and space. Interactive art is the 'happening' of the interface.

Söke Dinkla argues that most interactive art aims to 'socialise' the relationship between the recipient and the computer system (Dinkla 1997: 8). Interactive art is a social phenomenon in which the way the viewer encounters the work of art *is* the work of art. It is 'the *dialogue with the system* that becomes *artistic material*' (*ibid*.: 41, original emphases). Interactive art is therefore constituted both by the encounter, grounded in time and space, and the dynamics of that encounter, the actual event of art. Furthermore, interactive environments often have no guidelines (*ibid*.) and it is left to the viewer either to operate the work of art by entering into some kind of dialogue with it, or simply to maintain a discreet distance by choosing, for instance, just to observe the work of art in is objecthood, or to observe another viewer observing or activating it. Interactive art viewers are therefore 'at the same time spectators and actors' (*ibid*.). Negotiating between the real and the virtual, viewers are paradoxically both acting within the work of art while also looking upon it from the outside, hence producing an encounter in which the viewer is able to encounter themself, encountering the work of art.

The Australian artist Jeffrey Shaw indicates that there are a number of conditions within which interactive art often takes place: first, that the environment or room within which it takes place is presented as 'meta-architecture', and a 'labyrinth' which somehow functions as a 'mirror of the objective world'; second, that the virtual space functions as a 'theater of memory'; and, third, that the 'technological deconstruction' and 'artistic reconstruction' of identity work in 'surreal multiplicity' and as 'pathological consequence' (Shaw in Hünnekens 1997: 47). Under these conditions not only does inter-active art present the viewer with an environment within which the encounter between viewer and viewed takes place, but it constructs a new environment within which viewer and viewed again encounter each other in the virtual. In this sense, interactive art is always meta-architectural, its path functioning as a labyrinth in that there often are no clear paths and exits, only entrances. In contrast to much post-modern art, interactive environments are also 'theaters of memory', not only in that they represent other, often existing environments (hence constituting, however distortedly, 'mirrors of the objective world') but because, like computer games, they allow the user to proceed, time and again, by trial and error. Finally, interactive art offers no unifying psychological principle but, on the contrary, allows multiplicity and diversity. In this sense, interactive art is the open artform in that it is ultimately the viewer and the viewer alone who is responsible for the 'performance' of the work of art.

Figure 3 The Legible City, Jeffrey Shaw, interactive installation, 1988–91, © Jeffrey Shaw, Media Museum, ZKM/Centre for Art and Media Karlsruhe.

Shaw's proposition that the interactive environment should consist of a meta-architecture and a labyrinth is clearly noticeable in his own work, *The Legible City* (1988–91), an interactive installation in which the spectator, by riding a fixed bicycle, can move across the virtual cities of New York, Amsterdam and Karlsruhe. Here the cities' architectures appear as letters and texts, and it is through the real movement of cycling that the 'city text' is penetrated further and further (Schwartz 1997: 149). The Manhattan version of this work (1989) comprises eight fictional storylines with monologues from New York's former mayor Ed Koch, Frank Lloyd Wright, Donald Trump, a tour guide, a confidence trickster, an ambassador and a taxi-driver (Duguet, Klotz and Weibel 1997: 129). The Amsterdam (1990) and Karlsruhe (1991) versions, in contrast, contain letters that are scaled and in proportion with actual buildings 'resulting in a transformed representation of the actual architectural appearance of these cities' (*ibid.*). Each textual line has a different colour so the viewer can easily follow a particular narrative path. Thus, turning the pedals determines the movement through streets that are constructed by letters whose form partially corresponds to the real topographical features of the three cities. Ars Electronica's jury statement describes the piece as follows:

> [t]ravelling through this city of words is consequently a journey of reading. Choosing direction, choosing where to turn, is a choice of the storylines and the user's position. In this way this city of words is a kind of three-dimensional book which can be read in any direction, and where the spectators construct their own conjunction of texts and meanings as they bicycle their chosen path there.
>
> (Ars Electronica in Wilson, 2002: 760)

Just as the viewer encounters the city in the darkness of the room, the city's borders are also engulfed by darkness, so that the viewer is immediately drawn into the light, towards the centre stage of this virtual world. The bicycle, almost hyper-real against the backdrop projection, is the medium by which the work of art can be entered and the journey begun. The process of reading thus becomes a journey in which different perspectives are visible: 'abstract constructivism, romantic distance and central perspective' (Schwartz 1997: 149). And yet, although itineraries of words, sentences and phrases should be possible, not only can one never really 'read' the text in its entirety, but the reading of smaller sections requires a persistent physical effort. The textual buildings are in a constant process of appearance and disappearance – by being too far or too close, their components, the letters, are either dwarfed by distance or appear as ominously gigantic skyscrapers, allowing for occasional reading but always escaping more complex interpretation. Invoking Michel Foucault's analysis of René Magritte's *Ceci n'est pas une pipe* in *Treachery of Images* (1929), Dinkla thus shows how the letters in *The Legible City* are also in a situation of 'not yet saying' and 'no longer representing' (Dinkla 1997: 122). As a viewer, one can go forwards or backwards, or even through the letters, cycling across this deserted postmodern wasteland – but one can never quite reach either knowledge or catharsis.

As in many other interactive works, there is only a point of entry, no exit, in this environment (*ibid*.: 115). The entrance denotes the moment when the viewer begins to exist in 'surreal multiplicity', torn between the real and the virtual. But the real and the virtual are not only in a relationship of opposition; they are in a relationship of co-habitation, as the virtual, in this work, also remaps the real. The viewer is therefore both present in Karlsruhe's real topography, and in the virtual, which remaps the real, so that they are able to travel through the virtual while remaining immobile within the real. As suggested by Lev Manovich '[t]hrough this mapping Shaw proposes an ethics of the virtual. Shaw suggests that the virtual can at least preserve the memory of the real it replaces, encoding its structure, if not its aura, in a new form' (Manovich 2001: 261). In this sense the viewer travels through topographic traces and by constantly repositioning themself in time and space acquire a sense of location and thus of significance. The virtual here intersects with the real, allowing for the possibility of metatextuality. Extending this, in *The Distributed Legible City* (1998) Shaw introduced a second bicycle that was simultaneously present in the shared virtual environment:

> [t]hey can meet each other (by accident or intentionally), see abstracted avatar representations of each other, and when they come close to each other they can verbally communicate with each other. In this way a new space of co-mingled spoken and readable texts is generated. The artwork shifts from being a merely visual experience into also being the context for a networked social exchange between visitors to that artwork.
>
> (Weibel and Druckrey 2001: 110)

Here, as well as in the original *The Legible City*, Shaw is not only allowing for the possibility of a virtual encounter, but is inviting the possibility of a spectator to this encounter, thereby transforming the activity within the interactive installation into a performance. Whereas the viewer of *The Legible City* experiences the process of cycling through the city as difficult, the viewer's spectator experiences it as comic, watching the viewer pedalling frantically on a small fixed bicycle going nowhere. Not only is the viewer therefore in constant negotiation with the work of art, which includes its virtual as well as its real presence in the environment; they are also themself, both virtually and in the real, the potential performance of someone else's reading of the metatext of *The Legible City*.

Similar dynamics are visible in the Japanese artist Masaki Fujihata's *Beyond Pages* (1995), which comprises an interactive environment in which a reader sits at a table. The environment is a half-lit room containing real objects: the table, the chair and a lamp. A book is projected on to the table, and against the wall facing the table are a projected clock and a projected door. By using a real pen to click on the virtual pages, the viewer may 'open' the book projection on the table and 'turn' its pages. 'Beyond the pages' are sound and visual effects: by touching the image of a pond the viewer hears running water; when touching an apple they hear an apple being eaten and see it disappear, bit by bit, each time a further page is turned. The

Figure 4 Beyond Pages, Masaki Fujihata, 1995.

viewer may also move a large virtual pebble across a page by touching it with the pen; hear the pronunciation of a series of Japanese characters; hear leaves rustling in the wind; switch the *real* lamp on and off by means of a *projected* switch; write on the steamed-up surface of a glass of water; turn a virtual sandglass which alters the time on the projected clock in the real room; and finally open a projected door to see a small projected child appear in the real environment and then disappear, while laughing merrily at something inexplicable.

As in Shaw's *The Legible City*, not only may the viewer, illuminated by theatrical light, be observed while in action by other spectators within the installation, but they may also be observed from a little window located on the wall upon which the clock and the door are projected. *Beyond Pages* also similarly functions as a meta-architecture of the virtual and the real, but clearly constitutes a double theatre with one spectacle being activated by the viewer/*performer* 'inside' the work of art and the other being observed by the viewer/*spectator* 'outside' the installation. The viewer, so focused on the virtual world, often appears to be unaware of being watched, and so of being the protagonist of this performance. A 'theater of memory' (Shaw in Hünnekens 1997: 47) in its own way, this piece also captivates via the sudden apparition of the child a moment of laughter that has long gone. Unsurprisingly many viewers repeatedly return to this particular page in an attempt to reactivate the child's laughter and thereby catch another glimpse of its effervescence, that ephemeral and fleeting moment of innocent happiness. Caught in another open work, the viewer of Fujihata's *Beyond Pages* travels through, backwards and forwards, both the literal and the metaphorical text of this work only to discover, if they can bear to look 'beyond the pages', that they themselves have become the text of their own performance, being watched by someone else, who sees them lit centre stage while they carefully negotiate between real and virtual objects, as they too are caught in a fleeting moment of marvel and curiosity. Yet again, it is not merely the virtual that constitutes this work of art, but the viewer's interaction with the interface that creates an event, and thereby becomes a performance for someone else to watch.

Neither Shaw's *The Legible City* nor Fujihata's *Beyond Pages* completely absorbs the viewer into the virtual, but rather both allow for a cohabitation of the real and the virtual that determines the main dynamic of the work of art. Not only is the viewer literally inside the work of art, but also, in moving from the real to the virtual and vice versa, they experience their own presence and absence and thereby constantly relocate themself, a process which in *The Legible City* takes place both topographically and metaphorically. It is this constant questioning and repositioning of identity, inside/outside, in time/space, both within the work of art and in relation to the body social, that constitutes the main action of interactive art.

Appearance and disappearance in Forced Entertainment's *Nightwalks*, *Frozen Palaces* and *Paradise*

Nightwalks (1998) is an interactive urban journey on CD-ROM produced by the British company Forced Entertainment in collaboration with the photographer Hugo Glendinning. Created with QTVR (Quick Time Virtual Reality) using photographs to build panoramic landscapes in which the screen can be turned through 360 degrees, *Nightwalks* allows the viewer to move across the streets of a 'fragmented' nocturnal city (Forced Entertainment 1998b). By clicking on specific images of objects or people, the viewer may move through the virtual environment and search for a narrative. They witness 'an "unseen" world of littered alleys and chained doors, strange patinas of orange light, empty streets and disused car parks' (Heathfield in Glendinning, Etchells and Forced Entertainment 2000: 22). The predominant colour, the patina of sepia light, gives the impression of being inside an old photograph, as if what is seen belongs in the past. By moving around the streets and looking for hidden dangers, as if the viewers themselves were walking down those alleys, a series of potential clues that allow access to other spaces are

Figure 5 Robin Arthur and Terry O'Connor in a scene from *Nightwalks* by Etchells, Hugo Glendinning and Forced Entertainment.

found. The first image encountered is that of the abandoned car park, the distant lights of the inhabited part of the city almost belonging to another world. By searching the car park, an unconscious, sleepy or possibly even dead male figure slumped in front of a lamp-post appears. By clicking on him, another street appears, in which a scarf lies abandoned on the pavement. By clicking on the scarf, and subsequently other clues, series of objects and ghost-like figures are encountered, such as, among others, a woman in an elegant dress; a couple stealing what looks like a secret kiss; a winged, angel-like female figure suspended against a wall; a couple copulating in a car; a man waiting for someone or something next to his car; a drunken half-dressed figure with the head of a pantomime horse dragging himself across the street. Because the clues function as gates to other spaces, the assumption is that they are meaningful in terms of the construction of the story. So, in order to move to a different section, or even reach the end of the piece, the viewer needs to search the pages for the clues, like a detective trying to piece together a case.

The image of the deserted car park that 'opens' the piece has a familiar quality, and through it the viewer becomes another inhabitant of this semi-deserted city. In trying to find the hidden links of the narrative, the viewer needs to move the cursor from one object or person to another, so that '[i]n place of a rigidly defined game or a single narrative to be "discovered", *Nightwalks* invites the user into an experience more akin to that of wandering, of trying-out versions of the truth, of making playful connections' (Forced Entertainment, 1998b). In this way, the viewer becomes not only a nightwalker, pacing the

streets in search of a story, but an active voyeur, looking, touching, even caressing the page via their cursor, in search of yet another clue.

The piece, 'both a distorted portrait of England and a catalogue of forgotten locations of an imaginary film' (Forced Entertainment 1998b), plays on an uncanny overlay of the 'real' (the recognisable locations) and the 'fictional' (the figures that are encountered). Through the use of QTVR, the recognisable locations appear as navigable (the viewer may move within them), while the figures are static (we may use them only as gateways). This creates a contrast between the active status of the viewer and the static status of the figures. 'In each of the *Nightwalks* scenes the events – from love affairs to fights and ghostly visitations – are halted at some banal or significant moment, while the viewer alone is free to move, explore and investigate' (*ibid.*). Thus the figures encountered are not only rendered as static, but are reified, so 'people themselves have the status of objects – strange clues to be found and connected in the otherwise deserted streets' (*ibid.*).

This alleged freedom of movement has been described as follows:

> [m]y experience of the world of *Nightwalks* is like recalling a dream where I travel through darkened streets, parking lots, and the overgrown waste-grounds that make me feel uncomfortable when walking through the city. This is a place of strange meetings and encounters, where the city becomes the backdrop for images of people kissing, a man stepping out of a car, a person streetwalking in striped pyjamas, a masked figure making a phone call, a woman on a street corner with angel's wings.
>
> (Quick 1999: 107)

It is precisely this creation of unease, the dream-like quality of the experience, that renders the experience of *Nightwalks* so uncanny. As Adrian Heathfield suggests, '[t]his is a city found after almost all the humanness has gone, remaining only the still figures that haunt the space and the material residues of long-forgotten actions' (Heathfield in Glendinning, Etchells and Forced Entertainment 2000: 22). In fact, in *Nightwalks* one encounters not so much the clues of an action as their traces. Andrew Quick sums up the experience as follows: 'I continuously find myself getting lost as I am brought back to a scene already experienced, where I click on another doorway or keyhole in the hope that it takes me in a new direction. As in the dream, I don't seem to be able to find an exit' (Quick 1999: 108). With no clear ending, clues that reveal themselves to be nothing but traces of a forgotten or non-existent plot, nothing 'happening' other than the action of the viewer, looking, touching, then looking again, *Nightwalks* does not allow the viewer to find a narrative other than that which is encoded in the act of viewing itself. A lone nightwalker, the reader is literally in the dark, interpretation always escaping them, however frantic and desperate the search may be. The only encounter occurring in this piece is that with the 'lifeless' images Glendinning creates that capture a sense of something long gone. Just like the 'real', the virtual world of *Nightwalks* is embedded with traces of narratives that escape holistic interpretation.

Forced Entertainment's earlier collaboration with Glendinning, *Frozen Palaces* (1997), also written on CD-ROM and created with QTVR, takes place indoors. The setting is a house seen in what appears to be the aftermath of a party:

> the starting point for *Frozen Places* is a series of panoramic scenes staged for the camera in a domestic location, each scene involving many 'characters' or performers. Photographed and then rendered as navigable panoramas using QTVR, the interlocking scenes of the work explore, as the title suggests, frozen glimpses of complex events.
>
> (Etchells 1999: 54)

Here, as in *Nightwalks,* 'the stillness is posed as a psychic problem' and, again, in a total subversion of the theatrical canon, 'the viewer alone is free to move' (Etchells 1999: 54). Furthermore, 'scenes migrate from people sleeping in the detritus of a celebration to dead bodies in the cellar, a woman clutching a knife over a figure bleeding into an old metal bath, from a seance to a threesome and a man naked and drunk in a bed' (Quick 1999: 108). As in *Nightwalks*, the event has already taken place; all the viewer can witness is its aftermath. 'The bullet has been shot, the corpse has bled, the party has long finished, the levitation performed, the sex is done' (Heathfield in Glendinning, Etchells and Forced Entertainment 2000: 22). Yet again, only by searching for and engaging with the leftover traces can the viewer move from one room to another. Peggy Phelan remarks: 'the event that comprises the dramatic action has occurred before the spectator's arrival. History has already happened and the spectator-witness is left to decipher its elusive causes and meanings.' (Phelan in Sommer 2002: 304). The viewer has missed the event and can only interpret its traces: 'like a detective or forensic scientist, I am impelled to construct narratives that might tie the images together' (Quick 1999: 108). So the viewer cannot inhabit the house but, like a latecomer, may only wonder what they missed. And yet, as Heathfield suggests, 'the experience of the spectator moving "through" these images is one of restlessness and non-belonging. The journey never ends and the object of the search is not found' (Heathfield in Glendinning, Etchells and Forced Entertainment 2000: 22). Not only has the event already happened, and the narrative, as in *Nightwalks*, can neither be completed nor fully grasped, but the viewer is obviously excluded from the seminal act.

Tim Etchells described the piece as a hybrid, a mixture of genres:

> [f]rom installation it takes the active, seeking and mobile gaze of the viewer in 3-dimensional (albeit virtual) space, from cinema it can reference the conventions of moving camera and point-of-view, and from photography it can allow us to render the world as a still moment, a place in which time has been halted.
>
> (Etchells 1999: 61)

It is precisely from the juxtaposition of these different genres – installation, cinema and photography – that the complexity of the vocabularies of the piece stems. As pointed out by Etchells, the world of installation and the very fact that the viewer is facing a seemingly interactive piece suggest that they are responsible for navigating, exploring and finally activating (and hence, to some extent, performing) the work of art. Because the piece is constructed virtually, the viewer experiences a cohabitation of the real and the virtual by which they simultaneously experience the physical sensation (via the acts of touching and looking) through the virtual location (the viewer is inside the work of art). The piece also uses the cinematic convention of point-of-view, so that the viewer not only experiences the work of art from within it, but perceives the spectacle as taking place in front of them and thus subsequently *for* them (the viewer is not simply an onlooker but the very spectator of the action). Finally, the use of photography allows for the inclusion of stillness so that the activity of the viewer is juxtaposed against the static quality of the figures encountered within the piece.

Heathfield recounts the interaction of viewer and work of art as follows:

> [t]he open resonance of the images and the absence of narrative structure clearly signal that as a spectator you carry a responsibility to make the work, by transforming its fragments

with your associations, sense and logic. However, you move by a simulation of animation within a dead landscape: the fictional worlds are suspended in a frozen photographic moment. What's important about the role of the spectator here and the use of space is that the freedom to roam that you are ostensibly given is shown to be prescribed, to be an illusion. Again the spectator meets the limits of representation, or here the limits of what can be seen.

(Heathfield in Glendinning, Etchells and
Forced Entertainment 2000: 21)

Although the perspective offered to the viewer of the event that took place in *Frozen Palaces* is that of the spectator, no spectacle appears to have taken place. What is witnessed may be nothing but an illusion. And not only may what is seen never have taken place, but the presence of the viewer themself, their experience of movement and freedom, as opposed to the figures' immobility, may therefore be the result of illusion alone. This performance of hypertext is most certainly constrained. Invited to navigate and make sense of this textual world, the viewer finds that their navigation is at best circular and that explanation is impossible.

Phelan claims that '*Frozen Palaces* gestures toward what is at stake, philosophically, in collapsing the boundary between the alive and the mediated' (Phelan in Sommer 2002: 303). It is therefore from the clash of live and mediated, and, more specifically, the clash between the possibility of movement innate in the construction of the work of art as installation and the condition of immobility derived from its existence as photographic still that the sense of illusion and estrangement experienced by the viewer originates.

In installation art, as well as in Net Art, the emphasis is on the viewer's capacity for and freedom of movement. The object is experienced or explored phenomenologically and the viewer exits the environment, whether virtual or not, having participated actively in the 'happening' of the work of art. Through installation art, the viewer therefore experiences their own presence and is able to relate their presence to the work of art, and vice versa. By juxtaposing this experience with the encounter of photographic stills, Forced Entertainment locates the viewer in a paradoxical cohabitation of the live and the mediated. Barthes has shown how the photographic medium not only transforms the subject into object, but into 'a museum object', in that photography is in fact 'a kind of *Tableau Vivant*, a figuration of the motionless and made-up face beneath which we see the dead'. Explaining how photography is about the 'That-has-been', he shows how a photograph is simultaneously a 'certificate of presence', a presence 'that-has-been' and an absence, a lack (Barthes 2000: 13, 32, 77 and 87). Barthes explains this paradoxical role as follows:

> [f]or the photograph's immobility is somehow the result of a perverse confusion between two concepts: the Real and the Live: by attesting that the object has been real, the photograph surreptitiously induces belief that it is alive, because of that delusion which makes us attribute to Reality an absolutely superior, somehow eternal value; but by shifting this reality to the past ('this-has-been'), the photograph suggests that it is already dead.
>
> (Barthes 2000: 79)

Looking at a photograph, Barthes shows, is therefore watching '*over a catastrophe which has already occurred*. Whether or not the subject is already dead, every photograph is this catastrophe' (Barthes 2000: 96, original emphasis). In *Nightwalks* and *Frozen Palaces*, the viewer is constantly lured into an experience of the work in which, however, they find nothing but a trace of a long-gone catastrophe that either took place in their absence or never took place at all. As suggested by Barthes, the photograph is a 'new form of hallucination: false on the level of perception, true on the level of time: a temporal hallucination' (*ibid.*: 115). Both *Nightwalks* and *Frozen Palaces* confront the viewer with a temporal hallucination, and it is precisely this hallucination, this illusion of representation, that produces the collapse of boundaries between the viewer's active presence (the live) and the representation (the remediated).

As pointed out by Etchells, the relationship between the spectator and the work of art is called into question here and a reversal of canonical interrelationships between time/space and character/performer/spectator is produced. The viewer's experience resides in the world of phenomenology. On the other hand, the encounter with the photographic still and the fact that the very encounter is happening inside the medium (inside the CD-ROM) catapult them into the realm of simulation. As suggested by Jean Baudrillard:

> [t]he photographic gaze has a sort of nonchalance which non-intrusively captures the apparition of objects. It does not seek to probe or analyse reality. Instead, the photographic gaze is 'literally' applied on the surface of things to illustrate their

apparition as fragments. It is a very brief revelation, immediately followed by the disappearance of the objects.

(Baudrillard 1999: 1)

So, whereas the viewer is attempting to experience the installation literally by navigating through them, the photographic stills encountered only present themselves as ghosts, brief apparitions that immediately vanish. Here, as in Gilles Deleuze's analysis of the Baroque, 'hallucination does not feign presence, but [. . .] presence is hallucinatory' (Deleuze 1993: 125).

In *Nightwalks* and *Frozen Palaces*, the work of art resides in the clash between the presence implied in the materiality of the live and the absence implied in its photographic, virtual and mediated nature. The event becomes in itself a contaminated space in which dialectical opposites clash. This clash, or confrontation even, between the viewer and the frame, produces a similar effect to that found in the confrontation between the lens and the object, which constitutes the photographic event. In fact, according to Baudrillard, 'the photographic event resides in the confrontation between the objects and the lens [*l'objectif*], and in the violence that this confrontation provokes' (Baudrillard 1999: 1). In this clash of the real and the mediated, this violence must produce a slippage. In the encounter between the viewer and the work of art in both *Nightwalks* and *Frozen Palaces*, the 'leak' is that which is beyond representation and beyond the possibility of encounter: the sudden perception of the possibility of one's own absence.

Another piece by Forced Entertainment exploring both metatextuality and meta-architecture, again through a clash of the real and the virtual, is *Paradise* (1998), an Internet project comprising an imaginary city with five boroughs. Orientation through *Paradise*'s long rows of cut-out buildings takes place by following the four cardinal points. Astrid Sommer describes the environment as follows:

[e]veryone is invited to wander around and explore the streets and buildings at the click of a mouse. One can even 'move into' a house by contributing a text, and discover the stories of other contributors by visiting their houses. The buildings were all vacant when the project was launched, inviting visitors to 'join the community' and make manifest through individual texts the fantasies and stories.

(Sommer in Glendinning, Etchells and
Forced Entertainment 2000: 8)

Paradise is a hypertextual container, an empty, ghost-like city. As suggested by Forced Entertainment itself,

> *Paradise* is the plan for a deserted metropolis, waiting to be filled. Each of its one thousand imaginary buildings is the location for some untold story, some unspoken dialogue, some as-yet-unmade theory, some unscrawled poem, some unlived life [. . .] *Paradise* invites you to explore – read its stories, search its streets. *Paradise* invites you to write – to fill its buildings, write its dreams.
>
> (Forced Entertainment 1998a)

A model hypertextual environment, *Paradise* is both textual and meta-textual, a real community and a utopia. But in *Paradise* 'no direct communication is possible among the contributors. Instead the texts and houses resonate the bygone presence of their visitor-occupants' (Sommer in Glendinning, Etchells and Forced Entertainment 2000: 8). As in *Nightwalks* and *Frozen Palaces*, the visitor experiences a clash between the live and the mediated, between presence and absence. It is within this clash, due to a series of illusions and simulations, that the live is no longer always identifiable with presence – as the viewer, in becoming part of the work of art, becomes temporarily absent to themself – just as the mediated may no longer be merely constituted by what is absent – as online the mediated, or remediated, is always also a symptom of someone's presence. It is this interplay of presence and absence interlocking the viewer into the experience of the work of art, or, better, into the experience of themself experiencing the work of art, that constitutes the most dynamic and fundamental characteristic of hypertextual practice, a practice which, by reproducing the game of the real and the virtual for the viewer, allows the viewer both to experience and see themself experiencing the work of art in an endless fractal chase of the real, the virtual and their representation.

2

CYBORG THEATRE

Cyborg theatre is an art form that uses cybernetics as part of its method and practice. Although the relationship between theatre and the machine is well established, this use of cyborg technology, in which the machine and the human cohabit, is new. Cyborg theatre is primarily concerned with the modification and augmentation of the human, yet is also about the enmeshing of the human with the environment, whether in the 'real' world or in the simulated world of the World Wide Web. Furthermore, cyborg theatre is about communication and control, expansion and conscription, freedom and imprisonment. Finally, cyborg theatre always takes place through and on the body of the performer, where the body itself becomes both the laboratory and the theatre of the piece. In this context, cyborg theatre not only allows viewers the possibility of entering the work of art, which coincides with the performer's body, but offers them the disturbing possibility of interacting with this body. As a consequence, even when cyborg theatre is not overtly 'political', it inevitably raises ethical and political questions reminding the viewer that ultimately they are responsible not only for the interpretation but also for the actualisation of the work of art. In cyborg theatre the viewer is drawn directly into the performance and thereby becomes the last prosthetic component, both literally and metaphorically, of the performer's modified body.

Constructing cyborg

While cyborg theatre is a contemporary phenomenon, the liminal space of cyborgs has its roots in the West's regulation of social and ethical 'norms'. Indeed, it is in such spaces that, Donna Haraway argues, 'monsters' have always defined the limits of community even as they have implicitly challenged the boundaries of society in Western imaginations. The centaurs and Amazons of ancient Greece established 'the limits of the centred polis of the Greek male human by their disruption of marriage and boundary pollutions of the warrior with animality and woman' (Haraway 1991: 180). Likewise, unseparated twins and hermaphrodites 'were the confused human material in early modern France who grounded discourse on the natural and supernatural, medical and legal, portents and diseases – all crucial to establishing modern identity' (*ibid.*). In both ancient Greece and early modern France, representations of 'monsters' have therefore acted as indicators of the boundaries of the human order. These organic ur-cyborgs not only worked as *other* to the human, but also acted as a space of liminality and therefore as an invisible human prosthetic reaching out towards the unknown.

While 'monsters' have played a major role in both Western and non-Western imaginations, the Western world has also produced another liminal figure key to the conception of the cyborg: that inhabited by the automaton. Norbert Wiener presented a history of automata that was divided into four stages, each corresponding to a specific concept of the body in relation to the machine: a 'mythic Golemic age'; 'the age of clocks' (seventeenth and eighteenth centuries); 'the age of steam' (eighteenth and nineteenth centuries); and finally 'the age of communication and control' (Wiener 1948: 50–1). Wiener believed that these stages generated four models for the human body: the body as a malleable, magical clay figure; the body as a clockwork mechanism; the body as a 'glorified heat engine'; and the body as an electronic system (*ibid.*: 1). Whereas Haraway's centaurs and Amazons belong to Wiener's golemic age, the first representations of machinic monsters are found in the seventeenth and eighteenth centuries, and what is often considered to be the first cyborg, Mary Shelley's Frankenstein's monster, was created only in 1818, during Wiener's 'age of steam'. The cyborg is a creation of the twentieth century, Wiener's 'age of communication and control', and most fiction, whether literature, film or performance, presents it as the product of the interrelationship between these two factors.

But before cyborgs appeared, another 'monster' came to life which had characteristics that were to prove profoundly influential in the creation of the cyborg: namely, the robot which made its debut in Karel Čapek's play *R.U.R.* in 1923. This complex figure marks the emancipation of technology in relation to previous ages. Here, the technological has come to life and the machine has become a plausible alternative to the human. Throughout the twentieth century the robot entered the 'real' world. In 1947, just over two decades after

Čapek's creation, the word 'automation' first appeared at the Ford Motor Company (Huhtamo in Lunenfeld 2001: 100), and in 1955 Plantbot – the first robot to be used industrially by General Motors (Giannetti 1998: 8) – emerged. Thus, throughout the second part of the twentieth century, scary robots became friendly bots, and automata became increasingly integrated into methods of mass production, both culturally and socially.

While the robot was developing, in 1947 a new science, cybernetics, which intended to unite communications theory, control theory and statistical mechanics, was born. The word was derived from the ancient Greek for steersman (Wiener 1948: 19), so inherent in the concept of cybernetics is navigation, which, as in the case of hypertext, also implies the idea of a journey, of travel. The word 'cyborg' itself was proposed by Manfred E. Clynes and Nathan S. Kline in 1960 to indicate how the self-regulatory control function of individuals could be extended to adapt to new (extraterrestrial) environments (Clynes and Kline in Gray 1995: 31). Thus 'cyborg' also implied otherness, that which is not human. The first living being to be termed a cyborg was a white laboratory rat at New York's Rockland State Hospital (Haraway in Gray 1995: xi). The rat was implanted with a minute osmotic pump which injected chemicals into its body at a controlled rate to alter its physiological parameters. This was the world's first organism in which the organic and the machinic had been perfectly welded, so that what had 'evolved' and what had been 'developed' were not colliding but cohabiting in intriguing and yet perfect harmony.

Cyborgs have been variously defined as 'the melding of the organic and the machinic, or the engineering of a union between separate organic systems' (Gray, Mentor and Figueroa-Sarriera in Gray 1995: 2); 'a self-regulating human–machine system' (Featherstone and Burrows 1995: 2); or any of us who have an artificial organ (Gray, Mentor and Figueroa-Sarriera in Gray 1995: 2), have artificial limbs or pacemakers, have been programmed to resist disease through immunisation, or even wear glasses or hearing aids. Undoubtedly, with the appearance of the cyborg, the dividing line between the natural (the biological, the organic) and the human-made (the technological, the artificial) that had underpinned philosophical and socio-political thought for centuries began to blur. Cyborgs, like centaurs, Amazons and golems, represent the liminal zone of the human. But the realisation that cyborgs did not represent humanity's future, but rather defined its present, implied that humanity itself already contained the characteristics of its own transcendence. Since the vast majority of human beings are already cyborgs, the human is already super-human. This condition which defined our physical being also affected other areas of our life, since, '[w]hatever else it is, the cyborg point of view is always about communication, infection, gender, genre, species, intercourse, information and semiology' (Haraway in Gray 1995: xiv). In fact, the world of the cyborg, even more than that of the robot, was to condition both the literary and the social reality of the Western world.

Haraway gave the most enlightening definition of the cyborg when stating that '[it] is a cybernetic organism, a hybrid of machine and organism, a creature of social reality as well as a creature of fiction' (Haraway 1991: 149). This definition presented the cyborg not only as a hybrid of organic, biological and non-organic forms, but as a creature able to bridge the gap between the real and representation, between social reality and fiction. As Katherine Hayles suggests, cyborgs thus became both 'entities and metaphors, living beings and narrative constructions' (Hayles in Gray 1995: 322). In cyborg, the real and discourse cohabit. Haraway also pointed out that cyborgs are 'the illegitimate offspring of militarism and patriarchal capitalism, not to mention state socialism' (Haraway 1991: 151). Although she stated that cyborgs have been 'unfaithful to their origins' (*ibid*.: 151), in that they developed an explicitly political, even rebellious 'personality', cyborgs also maintained fearful characteristics, not only because they incarnate 'conflicting visions of power and powerlessness' (Cavallaro 2000: 46), but also because they still fulfil the same function as the centaurs and Amazons of ancient Greece. Thus, cyborgs are still the ultimate frontiers, beyond which the human is no longer recognisable as such. Paradoxically, cyborgs are therefore both human and not human: '[t]he cyborg embodies two opposite fantasies: that of the pure body and that of the impure body' (*ibid*.: 47).

Mike Featherstone and Roger Burrows point out that whereas the Clynes/Kline cyborg was conceived of as a 'superman', 'capable of surviving hostile non-earth environments', Haraway's cyborg 'was the product of late-capitalist earth' (Featherstone and Burrows 1995: 36). Thus, whereas the former cyborg was the product of the United States' space programme and a medical research laboratory, the latter was the product of mid-1980s political and feminist activism (*ibid*.: 37). So the cyborg is a liminal creature, both a superman (or super-woman) able to survive in unfriendly surroundings and likely to overcome medical conditions that the human alone could not endure, *and* a symbol of political (and especially feminist) resistance. Yet the cyborg also represents the frontier of what it means to be human, and thereby constitutes the borderline of what is socially, politically and ethically acceptable. The cyborg must, therefore, 'be exiled or destroyed in order to cleanse the community of its tendency toward violent protectionism' (Case 1996: 96). Thus, while on the one hand the notion of the cyborg 'aids the constitution of human, amplifying its possibilities' (*ibid.*), on the other, in the cyborg world, one 'seeks an identity that is partial, contradictory, [a] provisional construction' (Gaggi 2000: 18). The strength of the idea of the cyborg lies therefore not only in its hybridity of human (organic) and non-organic but also in the subsequent impossibility of reading the cyborg as a finite and easily classifiable creature. Thus, implicit in the notion of the cyborg is the idea of moving beyond the human. The cyborg not only augments and extends the human, both prosthetically and metaphorically, but allows for a new relationship with the environment. The hypertexted bodies of cyberculture are not merely interfaced to the Net, but have 'become *nets* in their own right' (Kroker and Weinstein in Cavallaro 2000: 29, original emphasis). Thus, a cyborg is not necessarily one entity. On *Star Trek*, 'a collective cyborg has already made an appearance: the Borg is represented as an integrated system rather than individualist cyborgs' (Case 1996: 102). The cyborg therefore represents not only the end of the human, but the end of individualism. The cyborg body is always already interconnected with its environment. In fact, it is read within its environment.

Cyborgs are intertextual and metatextual hybrids of human and machine. One cyborg does not necessarily correspond to either one body or one agency. Moreover, cyborgs are flexible, incomplete and fragmentary creatures. They are neo-Calibans. They are resistant to capitalism (Case 1996: 98), and they live 'in a post-gender world; [have] no truck with biosexuality, pre-oedipal symbiosis, unalienated labour, or other seductions to organic wholeness through a final appropriation of all the powers of the parts into a higher unity' (Haraway 1991: 150). Cyborgs represent the ultimate human aspiration to freedom while simultaneously indicating its end. They are paradoxical and uncanny: they appear to be setting a new frontier while pointing to something that was always already within. They appear to be enhancing our individual potentials while representing the end of the human as an independent individual. They are the product of Western imagination while also being part of its social and political reality.

In 'cyberpunk', the cyborg draws on both mythology and technology to emphasise the centrality of the body (Cavallaro 2000: xv). Thus, whereas in the 1960s and 1970s texts tended to depict how human minds were controlled by machines, in the 1980s and 1990s, 'the emphasis falls on the eternal night of apocalyptic megalopolies wherein abjection and monstrosity are *written on the body*' (*ibid.*: xiii, original emphasis). Here, not only is the cyborg enmeshed with the environment, but society's symptoms literally appear on the body, and thus the body becomes the palimpsest of society. Robert Longo's sculpture/installation *All You Zombies: Truth Before God* (1986) is indicative of the conflict of these dialectics. The figure is reminiscent of Ferdinand Victor Eugène Delacroix's *Liberty Leading the People* (1830) (Gonzáles in Gray 1995: 274) and represents a monstrous cyborg soldier on a revolving platform in what looks like a theatrical space described as a 'semiotic nightmare of possibilities' which stages 'the extreme manifestation of the body at war in the theatre of politics' (*ibid.*: 273). Jennifer Gonzáles describes the piece as follows:

[i]n a helmet adorned with diverse historical signs (Japanese armour, Viking horns, Mohawk-like fringe and electronic network antenna), the cyborg's double face with two vicious mouths snarls through a mask of metal bars and plastic hoses that penetrate the surface of the skin. One eye is blindly human, the other is a mechanical void. A feminine hand with razor-sharp nails reaches out from the centre of the chest, as if to escape from within. With arms and legs covered in one-cent scales, clawed feet, legs with fins, knee joints like gaping jaws, serpents hanging from the neck, insects swarming at the genitals, hundreds of toy soldiers clinging to the entrails and ammunition slung across the body, this beast is a contemporary monster.

(Gonzáles in Gray 1995: 274)

All You Zombies: Truth Before God represents the marking of the body through warfare and conflict. The result is the annihilation of the body as we know it. This cyborg is not only today's equivalent of the golem, the war machine, the robot, Frankenstein's monster, all in one, but the representation of the aftermath of the human. Thus *All You Zombies: Truth Before God* could be not only our nightmare but our end.

Unsurprisingly, one of the main fears in relation to the relationship between the human and the cyborg is whether the cyborg will ultimately surpass the human. Alan Turing and Hans Moravec have most famously explored this question. While the Turing test was designed to demonstrate that machines could perform thinking that had previously been considered to be exclusively a characteristic of the human being, the Moravec test was designed to show that machines could become the repository of human consciousness, that machines could 'become human beings', that 'you are the cyborg, and the cyborg is you' (Hayles 1999: xii), and consequently that the machine and not the body is the true repository of the (post-)human mind (Figueroa-Sarriera in Gray 1995: 132). So not only will cyborgs surpass human beings, but it is only through the cyborg that the human will survive.

We are, of course, *already* cyborgs, already enmeshed with the environment, already multiple and fragmented, carrying the signs of the disease of the social body, both the product of fiction and the real, always on the edge of death, always attempting to surpass it. But it is because we are cyborgs that we can shed further light on to what it means to be human.

The reconfigured body: Orlan and the operating theatre

The person who, by offering her own body as a site of performance, has most famously reinvented and even redesigned herself as an inter-text of myth, religion and art is the French performance artist Orlan. A hybrid of art and life, Orlan, whose name is also said to offer an intertextual map of possible referents (Ince 2000: 1–2), has since 1990 undergone a series of surgical operations entitled *The Reincarnation of St Orlan* to reconstruct her body according to somatic and symbolic characteristics from the history of art. Her forehead is from Leonardo's *Mona Lisa*; her chin is from Botticelli's *Venus*; her nose from an un-attributed sculpture of Diana by l'École de Fontainebleau; her mouth from Gustave Moreau's *Europa*; and her eyes from François Pascal Simon Gérard's *Psyche* (Ince, 2000: 6). The choice of references is not coincidental. Orlan selected Diana because of her insubordinate and aggressive character, and because she had leadership skills, whereas Mona Lisa was chosen because she represents as an emblem of beauty and because 'there is some "man" under this woman' (Orlan in Phelan and Lane 1998: 320). Psyche, on the other hand, was selected because she 'is the antipode of Diana, invoking all that is fragile and vulner-able in us', while Venus was chosen because she embodies 'carnal beauty'. Finally, Europa was picked for her adventurous character and her capacity to look 'toward the horizon' (*ibid.*). Defined within these networks of references, Orlan exists in dialectical tension between insubordination and aggression, leadership and manhood, fragility and vulnerability, carnality and adventure. She is not a creature of unity but one of fragmentation. In fact, everything about Orlan is artifice, from her name itself to her body, which remains a work in progress. Thus, in Orlan, the 'natural' is rewritten by technology, as she literally comes to embody that 'creature of social reality' *and* 'fiction' that Haraway describes cyborgs to be (Haraway 1991: 148).

For Orlan, every operation is 'like a rite of passage' (Orlan 1997: 39). Her transformation is post-naturalist – no longer does art imitate life. In Orlan, life imitates art. This ritual transformation takes place through the surgery, the remodelling of the body, not according to some fashionable conception of beauty but in an articulation of the body's intertextuality. Her 'skin is treated as a fabric to be cut, shaped and stitched into a new look' (Botting and Wilson in Zylinska 2002: 152). The skin, no longer simply confining the body, becomes the means for its transformation. Indeed, it becomes the *place* of its transformation and hence the site of the artwork. In the process of Orlan's operations,

> [t]he surgeon's drawing upon her face is quickly replaced by incisions, which yield lines of blood, which open folds in the flesh, create shapes, even forms that exist from moments when the face is detached – disembodied to be reformulated. It is this process, the decision-making essence of her art in action, that is most intimately linked to painting.
>
> (Moos in Orlan 1997: 10)

By drawing attention to the process of the making of Orlan, David Moos shows that the event of Orlan, the cutting of the skin, is in itself not only *an* art but *the* art of her 'Carnal Art'. Yet the viewer only sees the cutting of the skin through its mediation. In fact, Orlan exists in a state of constant flux. In other words, the artwork taking place is the very making of Orlan; hers is a condition of becoming, and the performance is the act of the transformation as seen through its mediation. Significantly, too, the making of Orlan can therefore be described as a continuous live and living performance. Orlan's body is a work in progress, hers is a fight against 'the innate, the inexorable, the programmed, Nature, DNA [. . .] and God' (Orlan in Phelan and Lane 1998: 325).

The first six surgeries of *The Reincarnation of St Orlan* took place in France and Belgium. The seventh, 'Omnipresence' (1993), was a multi-local phenomenon in that it was broadcast via satellite to thirteen galleries around the world, including the Sandra Gering Gallery in New York, the Centre Pompidou in Paris, Toronto's McLuhan

Centre and the Multimedia Centre at Banff. Sue-Ellen Case describes the piece as follows:

> [u]nder local anesthetic, with a woman surgeon, Orlan read aloud from a psychoanalytic text by Eugénie Lemoine Luccioni which posits, among other things, a notion of the body as obsolete. Orlan read before the knife cut into her face and two silicone implants were injected above her eyebrows to duplicate the Mona Lisa brow. She calls the entire project 'The Reincarnation of Saint Orlan', emphasizing, in a French Catholic way, the agency (saint) that resides in the changing body.
>
> (Case 1996: 117)

The title of the operation, 'Omnipresence', both alludes to Orlan's simultaneous presence, via the medium, in a multiplicity of locations and hints at the sainthood behind it, the agency and the act of transformation that is being performed. This creates a complex interplay of liveness and mediation, before and after, presence and absence, inside and outside. This interplay can also be read in terms of an exposure of the absence of a 'real' beneath or beyond representation:

> [d]uring her operation Orlan's face begins to detach itself from her head. We are shocked at the destruction of our normal narcissistic fantasy that the face 'represents' something. Gradually the 'face' becomes pure exteriority. It no longer projects the illusion of depth. It becomes a mask without any relation of representation [. . .] Orlan uses her head quite literally to demonstrate an axiom of at least one strand of feminist thought: *there is nothing behind the mask.*
>
> (Adams in McCorquodale 1996: 59,
> original emphasis)

In presenting the viewers with the inside, rather than the outside (an inside, however, that is totally devoid of psychology), Orlan not only subverts the canons of literary and performance writing but also that of critical theory. Thus everything in Orlan's transformation is meta-textual as well as performative. Each performance revolves around a philosophical, psychoanalytical or literary text and extracts are taken from writings by Eugénie Lemoine Luccioni, Michel Serres, Sanskrit Hindu texts, Alphonse Allais, Antonin Artaud, Elisabeth Bertuel, Fiebing, Raphael Cuir and Julia Kristeva (Orlan in Phelan and Lane

1998: 321). The operating 'theatre' also acts as a set: '[s]urgeon, atten-
dants, and observers [. . .] wear futuristic designer surgical gowns, as
does Orlan' (Augsburg in Phelan and Lane 1998: 305). Through this
performative set-up, Orlan is said to be able to 'defamiliarize and
desanctify conventional views concerning cosmetic surgery' (*ibid.*).
And yet, although the surgical event is set up as a performance, the
surgery itself is 'real', but the audience sees only its mediation. Thus,
'although the performance was "live" since it unfolded in "real time",
its "liveness" was not immediate but mediatized' (*ibid.*: 289).
Orlan, who also uses a sign-language interpreter 'to remind us that
we are all, at certain moments, deaf and hearing-impaired' (Orlan in
Phelan and Lane 1998: 315), is therefore presenting a real (a)live event,
which is part of a larger process of transformation, and consists of a
'real' surgery set within an intertextual and performative environment,
but which can only reach its audience through the very process of
mediation.

Naturally, Orlan's performance consists not only of the cutting
of the flesh, but also the 'finished product', the aftermath of the
operation. According to Orlan, Carnal Art oscillates between 'disfig-
uration and refiguration' (Orlan in Phelan and Lane 1998: 319). Thus,
it is also the remodelled body. With regard to this point, there are,
Orlan suggests, important differences between Carnal Art and its
predecessor, Body Art:

> [u]nlike Body Art, from which it distinguishes itself, Carnal
> Art does not desire pain, does not seek pain as a source of
> purification, and does not perceive pain as Redemption.
> Carnal Art is not interested in the final plastic results, but in
> the surgical operation–performance and the modified body,
> as venue for public debate.
>
> (Orlan in Phelan and Lane 1998: 319)

Orlan is intertextual in that she is literally 'made' against a backdrop of diverse readings and embodies a variety of intertexts, but the
phenomenon of Orlan also incorporates the audience's response. In
other words, Orlan *is* her own audience's reactions. She says, '[m]y
body has become a site of public debate that poses crucial questions
for our time' (Orlan in Phelan and Lane 1998: 319). Her body is
the site for the transformation and the object of her art. It is also the
site for the debate around her work. Thus the intertext of Orlan
incorporates the audience. Furthermore, 'Orlan performs a critique of
the change [of the body] while producing it. She is constructing a

critical performance of the imperatives of the regime of beauty that cuts into the flesh of women' (Case 1996: 117). So Orlan is process, work of art, audience response *and* its critique.

Her image induces a general pain, just as her performances provoke pain in the spectators: 'the performance slices through comfortable modes of viewing, representing a body in pain and causing a painful disturbance in other bodies' (Botting and Wilson in Zylinska 2002: 153). In response to the issue of the viewer's pain, however, Orlan recommends, '[w]hen you watch my performances, I suggest that you do what you probably do when you watch the news on television. It is a question of not letting yourself be taken in by the images and of continuing to reflect about what is behind these images' (Orlan in Phelan and Lane 1998: 315). In suggesting that the viewer should maintain a Brechtian distance within what is otherwise an Artaudian encounter, Orlan asks for the duplication of the presence of the viewer who is therefore required to be both part of and observer of the work of art. The circumstances surrounding Orlan's first public operation add a further dimension to this perspective. Orlan had to interrupt a symposium in 1978 to be rushed to hospital for an extra-uterine pregnancy and decided to record the operation in order to show it at the symposium in her absence (Augsburg in Phelan and Lane 1998: 286). She insisted on only a local anaesthetic so that she could observe the surgery being performed on her body:

> [h]er video performance consisted of Orlan's recognition of being seen in the act of observing the female self, since the camera recorded Orlan witnessing her own body cut up and exposed, as well as viewing the excision of a nonviable foetus from her own reproductive system.
>
> (Augsburg in Phelan and Lane 1998: 286)

Not only does Orlan therefore show her audience what is both an intertextual and a metatextual work, but she includes herself among the viewers of the making of herself as a work of art, thereby performing a twofold twist on the conventional relationship between the viewer and the work of art: first, she includes the viewer in the work of art by making the debate part of the work of art; second, she includes herself as a work of art, a performance, among the viewers, with both Orlan and the viewers allowed a double presence, as part of and as observers of the work of art. This multiplication of the roles of both the viewer and the artist within the work of art creates the possibility of a coexistence of multiple, even cubist, perspectives that challenge the significance and even question the very location of the artwork.

The making of Orlan is rendered yet more complex by the fact that she has also been involved in other acts of transformation, such as the eleven computer-generated images known as *Self-hybridation* (1998–9), in which her head is digitally hybridised with the 'head-sculptures, bone-structures, decorative prostheses and make up of Mayan beauties' (Ince 2000: 87). Likewise, in 1990 Orlan posed for a portrait photograph in which she wore the wig and make-up of the Bride of Frankenstein: '[w]ith pale face, full lips, a fixed robotic stare and an electric white weave standing out against the piled-high frame of hair, the portrait is a close copy of the image presented by Elsa Lanchester in the 1935 classic film *The Bride of Frankenstein*' (*ibid.*: 82). In this case, Orlan modelled her image on a fictional cyborg. As Julie Clarke suggests, '[w]ith her newly constructed chin leaning provocatively on her gloved hands, Orlan's pose draws our attention to contemporary constructions of the ideal and admired woman through the technologies of photography and film' (Clarke in Zylinska 2002: 40). This 'reincarnation' of Orlan is through the technological, and mediation is not only the means by which the artwork is broadcast but also its subject.

Haraway concludes her seminal essay on feminism and cyborgs by claiming, somewhat provocatively, 'I would rather be a cyborg than a goddess' (Haraway 1991: 181). Orlan presents herself as both a representation of a goddess, or even the embodiment of a *number* of goddesses, *and* a cyborg. What, in Haraway are still perceived to be polar opposites are unreconciled but cohabiting intertextualities in Orlan. She is becoming 'a sort of living palimpsest' (Auslander 1997: 131) and so the phenomenon of Orlan is made of layers of text, inter-text and metatext that include herself and the viewer in the work of art. Furthermore, Orlan performs the act of her own becoming, and not only in a theatrical sense but ontologically. The 'happening' of Orlan is therefore a montage of real and fictional, text and metatext, seen during their act of becoming, of transformation, and perceived through a process of mediation that exposes the failures of representation. In a sense, Orlan is a hyper-natural that has lost its referent to nature and become pure intertextuality. But Orlan is also public debate, showing 'the complicity of aesthetics, fashion, and patriarchy with the representational practices that define and enforce cultural standards of female beauty (e.g., painting, sculpture, surgery)' (*ibid.*). The cyborg Orlan is life and art, artwork and debate. Her theatre is an operating theatre – the place where life meets death without necessarily being suppressed; the place where the cyborg may be exposed in its making.

The performance of cyborg: the case of Stelarc

The person who has most widely experimented with the interdependence of the human and the technological, as well as the activation and even modification of the human *through* the technological, is the Australian performance artist Stelarc. By augmenting and extending the body, whether via prosthetics or the Internet, Stelarc (Stelios Arcadiou) has not only challenged common conceptions of the human, but radically redefined the interrelationship of art and society. In his work, Body Art meets Conceptual Art and both manifest themselves through the interface of the body and the technological. The realisation of this interface is the 'happening' of the artwork.

Described as the 'foremost exponent of cybernetic body art' (Dery in Bell and Kennedy 2000: 577), Stelarc has repeatedly challenged what is possible in the complex relationship between the human and the machine. His early works as a body artist in the mid-1970s saw him suspending his body via skin-hooks from cliffs and tall buildings. Talking about these works, he recalls that 'there was no desire to make the suspension a kind of image of levitation. For me the cables were lines of tension which were part of the visual design of the suspended body, and the stretched skin was a kind of gravitational landscape' (Stelarc, 1995). Already, in these works, Stelarc revealed an interest in the idea of augmenting and extending the body by using the skin as an interface between the 'inside' and the 'outside'. Whereas, in the suspension works, strings were used to challenge gravity and extend the body into space, the wires used in the later 'live' performances augmented the body either by allowing Stelarc to use prosthetic extensions or meshing his body to the Internet. In letting the artwork penetrate his body and in permitting external agents to activate the body, he has been testing the boundaries not only of art but of the very relationship between artist, artwork and viewer.

Whereas with Orlan the camera never goes too far beyond the skin, Stelarc has been working towards the inside. For him, the conventional relationship between the body and technology is reversed: the body is empty, hollow, a mere container of technology. In this sense the body is nothing but a medium. Technology, on the other hand, no longer just represents the medium but becomes part of what it means to be human. For Stelarc, 'ONCE A CONTAINER, TECHNOLOGY NOW BECOMES A COMPONENT OF THE BODY'

(Stelarc in Bell and Kennedy 2000: 563, original emphasis). So, Stelarc claims, 'I went within myself' (Stelarc in McCarthy 1983: 15). In *Stomach Sculpture* (1993–6), '[t]he idea was to insert an art work into the body' (Stelarc in Bell and Kennedy 2000: 565). As the hollow body becomes 'a host' to the object (*ibid.*), there were no longer any 'distinctions between public, private and physiological spaces' (Stelarc 2002b), and, '[o]ne no longer looks at art, nor performs art, but contains art' (Stelarc 2002a). In a reversal of the conventional understanding and use of inside and outside, Stelarc, through nanotechnology, brings the work of art, and subsequently the viewer, inside the body. When watching *Stomach Sculpture*, the viewer is therefore 'inside' not only the work of art but the artist himself.

In the project *Extra Ear*, initiated in 1997 and comprising the construction of an extra ear that could be positioned next to Stelarc's own real ear, 'the ear would speak to anyone who would get close to it. Perhaps the ultimate aim would be for the extra ear to whisper sweet nothings to the other ear' (Stelarc 2002a). Here, not only is the body augmented through technology, as is the case in Orlan's work, but the work of art and the viewer come to coincide *inside* Stelarc's own body. Of course, the ear is the organ of balance (Stelarc 2002a), and the creation of an extra one unbalances both the relationship between the viewer and the work of art and the relationship between the human and technology. The hollow body of *Extra Ear* is thus both host and augmentation, passive and active: '[t]hese performances are about technology viewed as a symptom of excess rather than a sign of lack' (Stelarc 2002b).

Stelarc's work is the unfolding of the interrelationship of the human and the technological. Always exposing the interface between the body, the environment and technology, '[t]he process is revealed, nothing is hidden' (Stelarc 2002b). Stelarc in fact always operates in an environment that is augmented through technology. He says, '[i]nterface technology is visible and quite close to me. Neither the structure nor the technology of the performance is hidden. My assistants aren't hidden either' (*ibid.*). Thus, in *Event for Amplified Body/ Laser Eyes and Third Hand* (1986), Stelarc used fibre-optics and lenses to demonstrate how the sensory and motor systems could be augmented through technology. This complex piece is an interactive performance 'that controls, counterpoints, and *choreographs* the motions of the virtual arm, a robot manipulator and an electronic third hand' (Stelarc 1997: 247, original emphasis). It 'combines real-time *gesture control* of the Virtual Arm, *pre-programmed* robot scanning *symbiotic* EMG activation of the Third Hand and *improvised* body movements' (*ibid*.: 247, original emphases). In other words, the piece consists of an overlay of robotic and human movement in which the latter can be both mechanical and improvised. Stelarc describes the distinction between the different types of movement employed in this, as well as in other pieces, as follows:

> [t]here are four kinds of movements in my performances: the improvised movement of the body, the movement of the robot hand, which is controlled by sensors in my stomach and leg muscles, the programmed movement of the artificial arm, and the movement of my left arm when it's involuntarily agitated by an electric current. It's the interaction of these voluntary, involuntary, and computerised movements that I find interesting.
>
> (Stelarc in Virilio 1996: 110)

Here, the viewer sees not only Stelarc moving, but a series of projections. These form a complex counterpoint to Stelarc's performance and are organised as follows:

> [s]ensors on the head and limbs allow the body to switch images from cameras positioned above the body, on the robot

Figure 6 Event for Amplified Body/Laser Eyes and Third Hand, Stelarc, Maki Gallery, Tokyo, 2 March, 1986. Photographer: Takatoshi Shinoda.

manipulator and from a miniature camera attached to the left arm – with the Virtual Arm being the other video default image. A relationship between body posture and images is established, with body movements determining the flow of images on the large screen – displayed either *singly*, *super-imposed* or in *split-image* configurations.

(Stelarc, 1997: 247, original emphases)

Thus the viewer of *Event for Amplified Body/Laser Eyes and Third Hand* sees a variety of more or less choreographed and voluntary as well as involuntary movements, from both inside and outside Stelarc's body. These affect the making of the external environment in which they themselves are immersed. In this sense the viewers are both inside and outside Stelarc's body, in that the environment in which they find themselves is ultimately drawn by and dependent upon his bodily movements and stimulations.

It is unquestionable that Stelarc's works are also about manipulation and control, as he admits: 'I see these performances as architectures of operational awareness [in which] ethical, feminist or political consid-erations are allowed to unfold' (Stelarc 2002b). He is not only in con-trol of a complex technological operation, but is also, paradoxically, being controlled by the very technological means he activates:

in the Internet performances even though half of my body was being remotely prompted by people in other places or by Internet data, I was actually actuating and controlling my third hand. So the third hand was a kind of counterpoint. People were being in control of my body but I was in control of my third hand and pretty much nothing else. And also the third hand sounds were amplified so I would actuate the third hand as a means by which I could compose the complexity of the soundscape that was being heard, and sound in a sense is the real virtual medium in that it immerses. I used sound not only to register a movement but also to allow an audi-ence to inhabit the physical body of the performer.

(*ibid.*)

This interrelation of control and controlled reveals itself as an inter-play of presence and absence which has been described as follows:

Stelarc's gaze became simultaneously active/passive, adding a new dimension to sensory perception and interpretation of his external space. The motor signals given off by his left arm provided information output to activate the surrounding installation, jerking in response to erratic muscle stimulations, while his prosthetic third arm executed carefully choreographed movements.

(Armstrong in Keidan 1996: 24)

While Stelarc has expanded his body by the use of prostheses and by interconnecting the movements of these with cameras, he has also limited the control he is able to exert over his body by allowing it to be partly activated by the machine. To let technology affect the body, Stelarc therefore has to 'absent' himself partly, allowing himself to be simultaneously active and passive, container and contained.

Through this more or less conscious interplay, Stelarc presents the disappearance of the human as a self-contained independent and self-sufficient entity and proposes a body which is always already in a relationship with the environment: '[w]e mostly operate as absent bodies. That is because A BODY IS DESIGNED TO INTERFACE WITH ITS ENVIRONMENT' (Stelarc in Bell and Kennedy 2000: 562, original emphasis). The body therefore 'BECOMES A SITE BOTH FOR INPUT AND OUTPUT' (ibid.: 567, original emphasis). Just as the outside interferes with the inside of Stelarc's body, the inside is projected outside to become part of the 'technology' of the performance itself. As in Orlan's work, the distinction between private and public, inside and outside, is made to dissolve:

> [a] welter of thrrrups, squeals, creaks and cricks, most of them originating from Stelarc's body, whooshes around the performance space. The artist's heartbeat, amplified by means of an ECG (electrocardiograph) monitor, marks time with a muffled, metronomic thump. The opening and closing of heart valves, the slap and slosh of blood are captured by Doppler ultrasonic sound transducers, enabling Stelarc to 'play' his body.
>
> (Dery 1996: 155, original emphases)

In *Ping Body* (1996) and *Parasite* (1997), this possibility of 'play' was taken a step further in that the artist's body was directly connected to and activated by the Internet. In *Ping Body*, described by Stelarc as 'an Internet Actuated and Uploaded Performance' (Stelarc in V2 1997: 27), the body became 'a barometer of Internet activity' (Stelarc 2002b). In this piece, Stelarc linked his neuromuscular system to the Net. The frequency and intensity of the pings drove his enhanced body and his neuromuscular spasms beyond his conscious control. For, in *Ping Body*,

> instead of the body being prompted by other bodies in other places, Internet activity itself choreographs and composes the performance [. . .] The usual relationship with the Internet is flipped – instead of the Internet being constructed by the input from people, the Internet constructs the activity of one body.
>
> (Stelarc in V2 1997: 27)

Exploring ideas of 'access and actuation, of hosting and of multiple agency' (Stelarc in Zylinska 2002: 120), Stelarc reverses the usual relationship between the user and the net by reducing the body to the status of an object. Likewise, in *Parasite*, a search engine was constructed which selected and analysed images from the Net and displayed them in Stelarc's video headset. The real-time images were then projected onto the body which was actuated proportionally to the incoming file sizes. Here, Stelarc discloses, 'the Internet is experienced more like a kind of external nervous system that optically stimulates and electrically activates the body' (Stelarc 2002b). And so, in this piece, 'the cyborged body enters a symbiotic/parasitic relationship with information' (Stelarc 2002a). Again the body became the interface between inside and outside, between an aesthetic of appearance and one of disappearance, between the individual and the Net.

Similar dynamics were also explored in *Telepolis* (1995), in which visitors to the Pompidou Centre in Paris, the Media Lab in Helsinki and the Doors of Perception Conference in Amsterdam were able to 'remotely access and actuate' Stelarc's body in Luxembourg by using a touch-screen-interfaced muscle-stimulation system (Stelarc in V2 1997: 23). Although the visitors thought that they were just activating Stelarc's limbs, 'they were inadvertently composing the sounds that were heard and the images of the body they were seeing' (*ibid.*), hence authoring not only the performance of 'Stelarc' but the very environment in which this took place. Again, it was the skin that acted as a gateway between inside and outside. With Stelarc it becomes clear that '[o]ur skins no longer demarcate a line between inner and outer except in the limited sense of the body's endurance. What is generated within the body as information is hooked into global networks' (Poster in Zylinska 2002: 28). The skin, thus representing the 'interface of the body with technology' (Stelarc 2002b), becomes the means by which the bodily architecture can be extended so that the inside can access the outside (via the projections and sound) and, likewise, the outside (whether work of art or even the viewer) can be allowed into the inside.

In *Fractal Flesh* (1995), Stelarc similarly interacted with the Net through an interface operating STIMBOD software, a touch-screen muscle-stimulation system that allows his body to be moved from a remote source (Clarke in Zylinska 2002: 49). This produced, in Stelarc's words, 'a body whose authenticity is grounded not in its individuality, but rather in the MULTIPLICITY of remote agents' (Stelarc 2002a, original emphasis). In this piece, which created 'intimacy without proximity' (Stelarc, 2002b), the viewer is no longer merely hosted in Stelarc, but becomes 'a parasite via the Internet [which is] safely hosted within Stelarc's body' (Gržinić 2002: 99).

Finally, in *Movatar*, Stelarc is planning a reversed-motion capture system. Whereas motion capture allows a physical body 'to animate a 3D computer-generated virtual body to perform in computer space or cyberspace', in *Movatar*, 'a virtual body or avatar [could] access a physical body, actuating its performance in the real world' (Stelarc 2002a). Thus, in *Movatar*, 'the body itself becomes a prosthesis for the manifestation of a virtual entity's behaviour' (Stelarc in Zylinska 2002: 129). In a reversal of the relationship not only between the inside and the outside, but also between real and virtual, Stelarc is proposing to construct what has been described as 'a kind of viral life form which will evolve in its interaction with the body' (*ibid.*: 128).

For Stelarc, the future is beyond the world of the skin, beyond locality and individuality. He claims, 'I don't think this means that we are becoming disembodied but rather that technology allows us to extrude and extend, extrude our awareness and extend our physical operations and the Internet becomes the medium through which the body can do this' (Stelarc 2002b). He also claims, '[w]hat it means to be human is no longer the state of being immersed in genetic memory but rather in being reconfigured in the electromagnetic field of the circuit – IN THE REALM OF THE IMAGE' (Stelarc 2002a; original emphasis).

In a world where the human can be altered both outside, via the use of medical technology, and inside, via nanotechnology, images, Stelarc suggests, can be imbued with 'codes that makes them more and more like viral entities'. These viral images 'have the potential for interaction and response' (Stelarc 2002b), they can 'proliferate, replicate, and morph' (*ibid.*). So, he concludes,

> there is the possibility that the realm of the posthuman may not simply be in the realm of the body or the machine but

the realm of intelligent and operational images on the Internet. Perhaps connected to a host body, these viral images may be able to express a physical effect and so the idea of a virtual and actual interface.

(Stelarc 2002b)

For Stelarc, as for Orlan (Orlan in McCorquodale 1996: 91), '[t]he body is obsolete' (Stelarc in Bell and Kennedy 2000: 562), because 'it is always outside the body that we find verification of existence. It is only through the cyborg that the body can survive' (Stelarc 2002b). In his art, the body is in need of technology, as it is only through the technological that the body can see and be seen inside out. In doing this, the body constantly questions itself by negotiating its relationship with technology and the environment. In a flattening of inside and outside, where everything is outside and the inside is no longer a private and inaccessible world, the body becomes an open and fluid entity that is always already enmeshed with the wider world, both in the realm of the real and on the World Wide Web.

The shock of the real: about pain, pleasure and Marcel-lí Antúnez Roca

The Catalan performance artist Marcel-lí Antúnez Roca, one of the founding members of the company la Fura dels Baus, has taken experimentation with robotic performance and cyborg theatre in a different direction. Whereas Orlan has remodelled her own body intertextually and Stelarc has experimented with the prosthetic and hollow body, both in real and virtual environments, Antúnez Roca has used robotics as a means to explore the encounter between the biological, both human and non-human, and the technological. His uncomfortable performance work therefore reveals what is possible through technology, in terms not only of the relationship between the viewer(s) and the work of art, but of presentation and construction of the artwork. The viewer is often empowered with the execution of the artwork, but where other artists have been more interested in exploring the aesthetic and artistic potential of this kind of interactivity, Antúnez Roca presents a more direct ethical provocation and exposes the political implications at stake in the seemingly playful interrelationship between the viewer, the performer and the work of art.

Antúnez Roca's early work *JoAn, The Man of Flesh* (1992–3) presented a nightmarish contemporary golem built to human size out of polyester and covered with real pigskin. His arms, head and penis moved according to the sounds generated by the viewers, and the piece was installed in a public covered market which 'fits in perfectly with [JoAn's] perishable, biological nature' (Antúnez Roca in Giannetti 1998: 53). In the project, which plays with the ambiguity of art, popular culture and the technological (*ibid.*: 9), an uncanny intertextual hybrid of non-organic and dead materials is brought to 'life' by technology. Claudia Giannetti recalls her experience of seeing *JoAn, The Man of Flesh* as follows:

> La Boqueria covered market in 1992. Although I wasn't exactly sure what it was – a robot, a puppet, an ad campaign product, a work of art – I spent some time observing the curious reaction of the public towards this 'being', covered in natural skin, which moved in accordance with words or the sound of the spectators' voices. Some people were having fun with the automaton's artificial movements, and patiently waited their turn to 'speak' with JoAn; others, seeing that the object's body was made of real flesh, made a hurried and irritated departure from the scene; while still others, like myself, were happy just to watch what was going on.
>
> (Giannetti 1998: 7)

The location of the piece, the market, suggests sellability, but also the old tradition of exhibiting individuals who were in any way different from the white European ruling class. The golemic aspect of the figure plays with ancient intertextual fears, and the fact that real skin is used adds an uncanny dimension to the piece. Yet, although the dreaded man of flesh is 'really' moving, coming to life by order of the viewer, he is also a victim. Unlike the fearsome golem of literary tradition, JoAn is encapsulated in an exhibition case, has only limited movement and has no will of its own. This man of flesh is a terrible reminder of the degree to which one human is able to control another. The market, the capitalist world, serves only to reduce the human to either a victim or perpetrator, or both victim *and* perpetrator.

In *Epizoo* (1994), the exposure of interactivity as a means of control was taken a step further. Antúnez Roca collaborated with computer artist Sergi Jordan to create an interactive installation/performance in which the artist's own body was wrapped in cables which the spectators could activate to produce 'real' pleasure or pain. Like Stelarc, Antúnez Roca allows his body to be activated by the viewer,

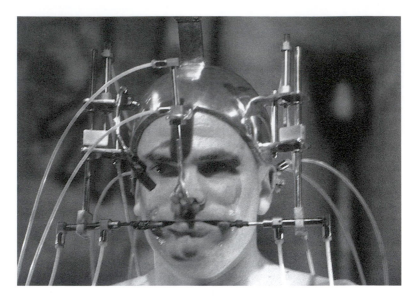

Figure 7 Epizoo, 1994, Marcel-lí Antúnez Roca, Estudi Marcel-lí Antúnez Roca and Luis Arellano.

and here the viewer's operation produces a visible physical output. As in *JoAn, The Man of Flesh*, the process of interactivity is exposed:

> [l]ike a living sculpture, Antúnez Roca places himself on a wooden platform. Pneumatically movable mechanisms are connected to nose, ears, glutea, and pectora. The audience is standing around the Spaniard while one of them is going to give pain or pleasure to the body draped in technology for the next couple of minutes [. . .] The person at the touch screen has started a rhythmical synthesizer sound [. . .] Without mercy, the person at the screen lets an electronic knife hack into it [. . .] It creates an ethical dilemma, because you are manipulating a human being and actually causing pain. In Mexico a couple of people turned off the computer, because they disapproved so strongly.
>
> (Wilson 2002: 160)

Through a touch-screen, the viewer may not only induce pain or pleasure, but also provoke sounds and create projected images, so producing, as in Stelarc's work, a larger environment containing both the artist and the viewer. These images 'lie between the grotesque and the monstrous, they mix fiction with reality, cruelty and irony, eroticism and obscenity, and are used as an interface between the artist and the audience' (Giannetti 1998: 17–18). Thus, the viewer not only finds themself involved in the actualisation of pain or pleasure, but in doing so they become part of a grotesque and monstrous world in which fiction and reality are no longer distinguishable.

Again, the politics of interactivity is exposed. The piece, Antúnez Roca suggests, is meant to create 'an ethical dilemma [. . .] I am not a sadomasochist. There are more important issues at work: the depersonalisation of human relationships, the blurred boundary between sex and power, and the use of computers as instruments of control' (DEAF 95 2002). In *Epizoo*, Antúnez Roca problematises the process of interactivity by exposing it as an instrument of control, and this affects the viewer as follows:

> [t]he audience here is not simply a voyeur, but rather is transformed, without realising it, into a kind of instrument of martyrdom. The fragile nature of the borders between pain and pleasure, between masoquism [*sic*] and amusement, between choice and imposition, perversity and the soulful, awareness and unconsciousness, etc., are clearly highlighted in the course of this performance.
>
> (Giannetti 1998: 17)

Lured into the mechanisms of the work of art by the 'innocent' prospect of yet another interactive game, the viewer quickly learns that any manipulation has direct physical and emotional consequences. Thus, Antúnez Roca claims that 'the action of the "remote agent" is an aggressive action, which can harm and even wound the body which is on the receiving end' (Giannetti 1998: 19). He also denounces the dissociation between the violence represented in the images and the significance of the violent act behind them, so, '[t]he spectator has, on occasion, lost all idea of his or her activity as the manipulator of the interface which makes it possible to move the devices attached to the artist's body, and, as a result, acts unconsciously as a torturer' (*ibid.*: 22).

As in the case of *JoAn, The Man of Flesh*, Antúnez Roca, the cyborg of this piece, is no more than a trapped exhibit whose emotions can only be induced. Incapable of any relationship with the viewer which is *not* the result of direct manipulation and control, the man from *Epizoo* is a dreadful reminder of what society could become in a world without reason. As the Brazilian artist Eduardo Kac commented, '[t]he longer a person spent operating the computer that activated

Marcel-lí's body, moving his body parts in an unusual ballet, it also became clear that the limited mobility of the artist was also significant in evoking the dangers of technologies of control. His body was besieged' (Kac in Giannetti 1998: 22). In Antúnez Roca's work, technology is both a means of movement and an instrument of torture; it is simultaneously a possibility for freedom and an act of repression. The viewer is always directly responsible for both the work of art *and* its political and ethical consequences.

A subsequent work, *Aphasia* (1998), is an interactive multimedia performance based on the *Odyssey*. The piece comprises fifteen sections ordered according to a visual index which functions 'as the interactive landscape of the voyage' (Antúnez Roca in Giannetti 1998: 73). Antúnez Roca is again a cyborg surrounded by screens upon which the viewer sees projections of cartoon-like and explicitly sexual images which respond to the performer's activities. The front stage is occupied by four interactive musical and mobile robots, among which is Antúnez Roca himself. He is the only performer in the piece, and describes his position as follows:

> I myself – the only performer – am equipped with an exterior skeleton made of plastic and metal, which is fitted to my body and allows me practically complete freedom of movement. This orthopaedic item works as an interface for the body, thanks to which the body's movements are converted into instructions for the computer. The exterior skeleton serves in turn as a support for small video cameras, microphones and several lighting effects.
>
> (*ibid.*: 70)

Antúnez Roca, who is 'both narrator and protagonist, both the "Homer" and the "Ulysses" of this Odyssey', is again 'defamiliarised' by the robots and the interfaces (*ibid.*: 74). As is shown by the title, the piece refers to the 'unstoppable transformation of the textual into the audiovisual' (*ibid.*). This incessant flattening of the textual world has been described as follows:

> the spectator sees virtual actors who appear and disappear, repeating actions over and over again, orchestrated by the only live actor-director, Antúnez Roca himself, who, armed with an exoskeleton, controls the images projected onto the screen, as well as the robots, the lights and the music.
>
> (Saumell in Giannetti 1999: 198)

The omniscient narrator of *Aphasia* has complete and final control over his world. Yet his narration is diseased, aphasic: words cannot be articulated or fully comprehended, judgement cannot be passed, the true nature of things cannot be represented. Here, the journey of narration, just like that of Ulysses, is circular. This journey happens only at the level of the interface. There is no link between the world of words and the real. There is only endless, circular representation.

Antúnez Roca's next piece, *Epiphany* (1999), was described as 'a space for in-depth reflection on the relationships between human beings and the worlds of biology (bacterias) [*sic*], technology (prosthesis, interactivity), culture (languages) and mythology (fiction and fantasy)' (Anon 2002). The work consists of four installations: 'Agar', 'Requiem', 'Alphabet' and 'Caprice'. In 'Agar', there are two Winogradsky columns containing anaerobic bacteria, some Petri dishes containing agar nutrients for fungi and a display with a fish tank for the cyanobacteria. What matters in 'Agar' is evolution seen as 'the process of transformation undergone by different bacteria and fungi cultures' (Giannetti 1999: 104). In fact, '[t]he Petri dishes [. . .] and their lifecycle provide a perfect example of this polarity between evolution and devolution, between dominant and dominated beings, between adaptability and inadaptability, between mortality and immortality' (*ibid*.: 192). What in previous pieces is seen at the level of the human interaction with the machine is here explored and made visible at the organic level. Thus the significance of 'Agar' 'does not lie in the solid objects of which it is composed, but in the ephemeral communities of micro-organisms which grow, reproduce and die' (*ibid*.: 104). The second installation, 'Requiem', comprises a pneumatic exoskeleton – that is, a mobile prosthesis – responding to the number and position of the viewers. 'By enveloping all the person's body, the system can move their jaws, shoulders, arms, elbows, hands, hips, legs' (*ibid*.: 191). 'Requiem' therefore 'reaches a point at which the body, converted into a cadaver, becomes ornament, and the machine is the only generator of life' (*ibid*.: 97). Similarly, 'Alphabet', the third installation, is formed by an octagon-sided wooden column containing a series of touch and pressure sensors. When the viewers touch or embrace the column, different voice recordings are heard. 'Anterior to the meaning of words themselves, these sounds give expression to different moods: desperation, anguish, pleasure, joy, tenderness . . .' (*ibid*.: 99). In 'Alphabet', it is therefore the machinic that ultimately 'speaks' the human. Finally, the fourth installation, 'Caprice', is an interactive piece formed by three statues and screens upon which images are projected, whose movement, size and position are again controlled by the viewers. Interaction happens through touch and voice, and varies according to the number of users (*ibid*.: 101). The title is a reference to Francisco José de Goya's etchings *Los Caprichos* (1799), which satirise the Spanish court, and therefore alludes to the possibility of criticism and satire.

Throughout *Epiphany*, Antúnez Roca invites the viewer to participate in the development and transformation of the artwork. Yet, by participating in the piece, the viewer also enters into the dynamics of manipulation and control that propel the work forward. Antúnez Roca thus subjugates the viewer to another odyssey from the biological world of 'Agar', to the technological world of 'Requiem', through the linguistic world of 'Alphabet' and ultimately to the epiphanic realisation of 'Caprice', which finally invites the insight that it is the power and duty of art to expose the ethical and political shortcomings of society. In *Epiphany*, as well as in previous works, the shock of the real is always a matter of politics, and, however disturbing the artwork may be, it is always the viewer's participation in the happening of the work that causes the greatest disturbance. In this piece, as in most cyborg performance, it is the human, not the technological, that raises the greatest ethical and political concerns.

3

THE (RE-)CREATION
OF NATURE

Nature is both the environment in which we live and a complex cultural construction. Hence nature both includes the human and is defined by it. It is both inside and outside the human subject. Because of this, there is an interdependence between the evolution of the human subject and the evolution of the concept and practice of nature. In recent years, through the development of genetics and artificial life technologies, the concept of nature has also come to embrace the genetically modified and the artificially created. Thus nature has come to incorporate what in its original definition it was not: the technological, human-made, artificially simulated unnatural. So nature is now inclusive of both the real and the virtual. It is both our 'homely' habitat and our *unheimlich*, uncanny surroundings. It is unstable and multi-layered because it is constantly changing as a result of our intervention. Nature, therefore, whether organic or technologically reproduced, is a means to expose identity and allow the viewer to see themselves performing as the 'other'.

The invention of nature

Technological progress has led to a revisitation of the concept of nature. As pointed out by Mike Featherstone, the division between the technological and the natural that has provided us with the key analytical categories used to structure and interpret the world is currently in danger of dissolving, and subsequently 'the categories of the biological, the technological, the natural, the artificial *and* the human are now beginning to blur' (Featherstone and Burrows, 1995: 3, emphasis added). Much has been written about this subject. In their survey of the field, Sarah Franklin, Celia Lury and Jackie Stacey (2000: 9) recall Donna Haraway, who claims that the differences between nature and culture have collapsed (Haraway 1997), Paul Rabinow, who argues that culture is the new model for nature and that nature has become equivalent to technique (Rabinow 1992, 1996a and 1996b), and Marylyn Strathern, who argues that nature has been assisted by technology to such a degree that it can no longer provide an ontological status which is prior to culture (Strathern 1992a and 1992b). Postmodern theorists such as Jean-François Lyotard (1984), Fredric Jameson (1991) and Jean Baudrillard (1994) have also been arguing that culture underwrites everything and that nature can be interpreted only as part of the world of culture. Far from representing a stable and unchanging parameter, nature and the natural, as well as all the various forms of naturalisms that have defined so much modern theatre and performance work, are therefore the results of a process of cultural construction rather than an 'original' state of the world. Invariably, as Raymond Williams has suggested, the idea of nature therefore contains 'an extraordinary amount of human history' (Williams 1980: 67).

As Franklin, Lury and Stacey argue, 'it has become commonplace to associate the present era with environmental damage, global warming, mass extinction of plants and animals' (2000: 19). In other words, we are living on a planet where nature itself as unaided, unassisted by humankind, is rapidly disappearing. The future of the planet therefore depends on our technological capacity to help 'nature' to stay as we know it. So the concept of 'nature' is no longer synonymous with evolution, in that evolution today primarily implies nature's capacity to adapt to a polluted and destructive environment. On the contrary, nature implies the preservation of the status quo or even the recreation of an idyllic, pre-pollution, pre-industrialised society. In this sense nature represents the past, not the future, of humanity. Humanity can preserve the past only by protecting it from the future or recreating it, artificially, as an artificial life system, a genetically modified environment, or even simply a protected and secluded environment as it is currently experienced.

Whether we agree with Katherine Hayles (1999), who argues that new reproductive and genetic technologies, such as cloning, call for a redefinition of the human as post-human, or with Franklin, Lury and Stacey (2000), who suggest that we need a redefinition of nature as 'reworked', nature clearly can no longer be read as independent from the human, and therefore as existing prior to culture. Rather, it is always already embedded in culture, and subsequently may be described as bearing traces of the human. Thus, not only does nature no longer provide us with a system that describes a pre-cultural, human-free condition, but it can be read only in terms of a cultural map of the human. It exists only as part of a complex cultural inter-text which, since the invention of artificial life systems, also includes the virtual within itself: 'nature becomes biology becomes genetics, through which life itself becomes reprogrammable information' (Franklin in Franklin, Lury and Stacey 2000: 190). Thus, arguably, not only do we live within the world of information society, but we *are* the information that comprises that world.

A good example of a human-made 'natural' environment is Biosphere II, which has been described as 'a model for the living environment of tomorrow' (Röetzer in Beckmann 1998: 134). Here, life is information and everything depends on the continuous control and monitoring of that information. It is

> a dome made of glass and noncorrosive steel grids in which the water, air, and food cycles are absolutely closed and re-cycled back into the system. Sixteen hundred sensors control the climate and the composition of the air, water, and ground, sending this data to a central control system. The computer network permits a continuous representation of environmental data. Inside the system we find, apart from some humans, around four thousand different species of plants and animals, not counting the microorganisms. Biosphere II is divided into five 'wild' ecosystems: tropical rain forest, savannah, coastal area, swamp, and a maritime area containing a coral reef. Beyond these there are farming zones and living quarters for the inhabitants.
>
> (Röetzer in Beckmann 1998: 134)

In Biosphere II, the natural, the animal and the human cohabit in a human-made environment that clearly attempts to reproduce the world on a micro-scale. Yet it exists only as a perfect equilibrium of data, an extraordinary equilibrium of virtual and real. This suggests that in Biosphere II, as in the 'real' world, organisms have become 'strategic systems', bodies that 'exist as a result of a continuous modi-fication in relation to their particular environments and the discourses in which they are embedded' (Becker 2000: 363). Yet, in Biosphere II, not only do the bodies and organisms modify in relation to one another, but they modify in relation to the body of information that is created and maintained virtually by the central computer. In other words, the human is both the creator and a performer of Biosphere II. Therefore, not only is this human responsible for the creation and maintenance of 'nature', but they are potentially responsible for the creation and maintenance of their own self. The human is always implied in the natural, just as the natural is always 'technologically' constructed by the human – as is suggested by Maurice Merleau-Ponty: '[w]e are caught up in the world and we do not succeed in extricating ourselves from it in order to achieve consciousness of the world' (Merleau-Ponty 1992: 5).

In recent years, the science of endophysics, which is a development of quantum physics and chaos theory, has taught us to look at systems that include the observer as part of the system and thereby show us 'to what extent objective reality is necessarily dependent on the observer' (Weibel in Druckrey 1996: 341). Endophysics points out that '[a]s human beings we are part of a world that we may also observe. Therefore we can only perceive it from the inside' (*ibid*.: 344). In the light of these considerations, endophysics postulates that '[a]n explicit observer has to be introduced into the model world of physics in order to make the existing reality accessible [. . .] Endophysics 'provides a "double approach" to the world. Apart from the direct access to the real world (by the interface of the senses) a second observation position is opened from an imaginary observer position' (*ibid*.: 342). Endophysics therefore offers a way of reading interactive art and process-oriented artificial-life art. Here, the viewer is often presented as both inside and outside the work of art. Through this 'double approach', the viewer is in the dispersed position of viewing themself while viewing the work of art. Artificial-life artworks and games therefore not only allow for the observation of a simulation of the real, but often include the viewer within them and thereby allow for the creation of complex levels of interaction between the viewer, the work of art and the environment in which both viewer and artwork are located.

Early artificial-life experimentations displayed only a basic degree of interactivity but already showed a fascinating complexity. One of the earliest artificial-life games was the *Game of Life*, which was invented by the mathematician James Conway in the late 1960s and was moved to a computer by Edward Fredkin of MIT in the late 1970s. The *Game of Life* is a simple two-dimensional grid of cellular automata in which each position or cell can be in one of two states: on (alive) or off (dead). Over time, cells are born when surrounded by three others; survive when they are surrounded by two or three others; and die if overcrowded (surrounded by more than three others) or isolated (surrounded by fewer than two others). From a random chaotic initial state the life grid starts displaying orderly patterns and finally complex multi-celled structures with dynamic behaviours. The extraordinary popularity of this game led to the creation of a series of variations of the *Game of Life*, such as John Simon's *Every Icon* (1997), which consists of a 32-by-32-square grid containing 1,024 smaller squares which display a neverending succession of calculated combinations. The top line alone has 4.3 billion variations that would take sixteen months to display on a computer operating continuously; the second line would take six billion years, so, of course, the game can never be completed (Rush 1999: 194).

The fascination generated by Conway's game indicated that artificial life would become an increasingly important subject for and of art. Not only was artificial life, in its capacity to simulate the real, offering an exciting model for a deeper understanding of the real, but it was allowing the viewer the possibility of a double approach whereby they could simultaneously be in a phenomenological rapport with both virtual and real environments. Finally, artificial-life models allowed the viewer the possibility to enter into the complex and rewarding experience of both perceiving the world through simulation and self-perception through pretended otherness.

At the Ars Electronica Festival in 1992, which was dedicated to the presentation of artificial life as art, Peter Weibel introduced the term 'Genetic Art' for works which simulated processes of life through technology (Weibel in Wilson 2002: 56). Well-known examples of Genetic Art are Karl Sims's *Galapagos* (1997) and Thomas Ray's *Tierra* (1991), presenting a simulation of evolution, and Ulrike Gabriel's *Perceptual Arena* (1993), in which viewers were able to evolve artificial-life organisms interactively. Other works re-presenting the natural have been aiming to introduce remote participation and telepresence into the development of natural micro-environments. A well-known example is Ken Goldberg and Joe Santarromana's *The Telegarden* (1994), which comprises a small garden at the Ars Electronica Centre at Linz containing an industrial robotic arm that is controlled by the Web and allows remote participants to plant seeds and water the plants created in the garden.

Interestingly, the study of artificial-life environments has shown that not all artificial life has been planned at the point of the creation of its environment. The decentralisation of intelligent computer networks around the globe has been producing independent software objects known as 'demons' that already display a tendency to form societies that resemble insect communities or economic markets (De Landa 1991: 121–2). John Frazer describes experimentation with built environments that are capable of sustaining the symbiotic behaviour and metabolic balance characteristic of natural environments and are subject to principles of morphogenesis, genetic coding, replication and selection. In one of these experiments,

> [t]he exhibition travelled globally by replicating itself in other host computers where, under different environmental conditions, the model is still diversifying. New genes developed on other sites could be fed back to the host computer in London which now holds a pool of biodiversified genetic material.
>
> (Frazer 1995: 79)

On one side, mankind is negotiating around new ways of defining and understanding nature that no longer separate nature and culture and no longer understand the natural as pre-technological. On the other, mankind is creating increasingly complex artificial-life systems that are able to interact with real environments and may even include the human within them. This interactivity produces a fluidity between the natural and the technological, the organic and the machinic, life and artificial life, so that the concept and practice of nature are constantly being redefined to include the cultural, the technological and the genetically modified. Nature is not a stable environment, but rather an evolving and continuously modifying overlay of the real and the cultural in which neither has the upper hand, but in which technology is the greatest human aid for the practice, maintenance, comprehension and recreation of the 'natural'.

The performance of A-life: Christa Sommerer and Laurent Mignonneau's interactive plant systems

The Austrian artist Christa Sommerer and the French artist Laurent Mignonneau have been collaborating since the early 1990s to experiment with interactive plant systems that allow the viewer to become the creator of the work of art. In 1992, they started to work with 'natural interfaces' and 'evolutionary image processes linked to interaction', leading them to create 'process-oriented art rather than pre-designed, predictable and object-oriented art' (Sommerer and Mignonneau 1999: 165). It was the latter idea that inspired them to develop works in which not only could the viewer interact with and even create the work, but the artwork thus created could improve itself even after the interaction had finished. So, in Sommerer and

Figure 8 Interactive Plant Growing, © 1992 Christa Sommerer and Laurent Mignonneau, collection of the ZKM Mediamuseum, Karlsruhe.

Mignonneau's interactive plant systems, the work of art becomes an independent micro-ecological system, created by the viewer and yet able to survive them and evolve independently from them.

Sommerer and Mignonneau's *Interactive Plant Growing* (1993) was the first interactive installation that did not use a device such as a mouse or a joystick, but rather allowed for interaction by means of touch. The piece consisted of an interaction between five real plants and five or more human viewers who could control the growth of a number of artificial plants by touching the real ones. Through the real-plant interface, the viewers could therefore determine what kind of plants should grow – whether ferns, mosses, vines or trees – and also affect the plants' size, shape and colour: 'the subtle personality and interaction differences of the visitors could be interpreted in the form of complex scenery that solely depended on each viewer's identity' (Sommerer and Mignonneau 1999: 166). Not only could the viewer of *Interactive Plant Growing* therefore produce their own artwork, but they could create it uniquely, so that each environment would constitute a visual map of both the viewer's position within the installation and their participation in it. The viewers entered a 'human–plant communication' that was translated into the virtual growth visible on the computer display (Sommerer and Mignonneau 1998: 151).

Interestingly, the interaction was presented theatrically. Upon entering the darkened room, the viewer faced five lit plants, behind which was a blank screen. On touching the plants the viewer activated the virtual growth upon the screen. This manifested itself as an explosion of colour akin to that produced by a firework. Without the viewer's interaction, the virtual plants first stopped growing and finally ceased to exist. The images disappeared as soon as the visitors left the installation and so the illusion lasted only as long as there was a viewer in the room. Inspired by John Cage's use of chance in musical composition, Sommerer and Mignonneau thus allowed random interaction to effect artificial evolution. Moving away from naturalistic objectives such as the mimesis or even the simulation of nature, Sommerer and Mignonneau aimed to 'apply [. . .] the A-Life principle to art projects' (Sommerer and Mignonneau 1999: 166) and herewith to create artworks that were able to manifest themselves as evolutionary processes.

In their subsequent piece *A-Volve* (1994), the result of a collaboration with the scientist Ray, Sommerer and Mignonneau created an interactive computer installation that allowed viewers to generate virtual three-dimensional creatures that lived in a water-filled glass pool. Viewers could design any kind of shape with their fingers on a touch-screen and so 'give birth' to a number of artificial organisms (Sommerer and Mignonneau 1998: 152). These would manifest themselves in the pool of real water, and the viewers could interact with them there through touch. As with *Interactive Plant Growing*, the creatures were the product of evolutionary rules and could be influenced by human manipulation:

> [e]ach creature moves, reacts, and evolves according to its form, creating unpredictable and always new lifelike behaviour. Since the organisms will capture all slightest movements of the viewer's hand in the water, the form and behaviour of these organisms will change constantly.
>
> (Sommerer and Mignonneau in
> Wilson 2002: 357)

Not only could the creatures change in response to manipulation; they could also mate and produce offspring with their genetic imprint. The offspring could then also live in the pool and interact with both visitors and other creatures. The three main parameters that regulated the interaction, reproduction and evolution of the creatures were fitness, energy and lifespan. The other parameters were external, and included the viewer's original drawing technique and their interaction with the creatures in the water (Sommerer and Mignonneau 1999: 168). Behaviour in space was an expression of the creature's form, which in turn was a symptom of their ability to adapt to the environment. The creatures' ability to move was determinant in deciding their fitness within the pool, so that the fittest creature would survive longest and would be able to 'mate and reproduce'. It was also recognised that the creatures were generally competitive and that 'predator creatures will hunt for prey creatures, trying to kill them' (Sommerer and Mignonneau 2000). Here, 'as in quantum physics, the entities transform their states according to probability patterns' (Sommerer and Mignonneau 1999: 168). Hence, in *A-Volve*, the environment featured A-Life principles 'in the birth, creation, reproduction *and* evolution of its artificial creatures' (*ibid.*: 167, emphasis added). As in *Interactive Plant Growing*, the virtual originated by the viewer, but it was also able to 'outlive' the time of the interaction: the life of the virtual creature was dependent on the original interaction with the viewer *and* chance encounters with other members of its 'species', which in turn had been created by other viewers at different points in time.

In 1995, Sommerer and Mignonneau developed an installation called *Trans Plant*, in which, by entering a semicircular room, viewers became part of a virtual jungle that appeared on a screen in front of them. Here, plants grew with each step the viewers took, depending on the size, colour, and shape of each individual participant:

> [b]ecause each visitor creates different plants, the result on the screen is one's own personal forest that expresses one's personal attention and feeling for the virtual space. As the growth gets more and more dense and the space more and more full of different plant species, the visitor also becomes deeply engulfed in this virtual world.
>
> (Sommerer and Mignonneau 1999: 169)

As in their previous works, Sommerer and Mignonneau created an interface that made the viewer directly responsible for the universe surrounding them. Like a magic mirror, *Trans Plant* literally transplants the participant into another reality in which they appear as a projection surrounded by the very plants that they themself created. Here, the viewer is simultaneously inside and outside, both in the real, as a perceiving body, and in the virtual A-Life system, flattened into the world of the image.

Different dynamics were explored in *Phototropy* (1994–7), where viewers could interact with virtual insects. This piece was based on organisms' tendency to follow light in order to find nutrition, so viewers were given lamps that induced computer-generated insects to fight for food. When the insects received sufficient light, they could reproduce. However, insects that stayed in the heat produced by the beam for too long ceased to exist.

> The visitor has to be careful with his lamp. Though it is very easy to use (a normal torch lamp functions as interface), it requires the viewer's responsibility and care for the creatures. If he moves too fast, the insects will hardly follow, and thus will have no time and occasion for reproduction. If he moves the lamp too slowly, the insects will reproduce rapidly, but reach the center of the beam too quickly: hence they will burn and die as fast as they were born [. . .] To really appreciate the creation and the development of new populations and individuals, the viewer becomes responsible for their creation, their evolution, and their survival.
>
> (Sommerer and Mignonneau in
> Wilson 2002: 357)

The viewers of *Phototropy* were no longer simply responsible for the creation of the work of art, but were in charge of its survival. Here, the viewer's real physical movements had direct consequences for the organisms in the virtual environment, thereby creating a micro-environment that existed right at the point of interface of the real and the virtual.

In discussing their subsequent piece *Genma* (1996), described as a 'dream machine' enabling users to manipulate artificial nature on a micro-scale (Sommerer and Mignonneau 1999: 170), the artists claim that '[t]he visitors to the installation themselves function as randomising factors, giving the artwork a particular form and development' (Sommerer and Mignonneau in Stocker and Schöpf 1996: 295). Through a glass window, viewers could see a number of projected creatures. By putting both hands into the glass box, they could grasp the creatures, manipulate their genetic code, and so change and modify their appearance (*ibid.*). So, 'one could say that the visitors themselves become part of the resulting artwork' (Sommerer and Mignonneau 1999: 173). The A-Life system, appearing to the viewer theatrically, through a window, incorporated the viewer as a randomising factor, which suggests that the viewer here was never really outside the artificial world but always inside what they themselves had created.

Experimentation with the interplay of real and virtual spaces was taken a step further in *Life Spaces* (1997),

> an evolutionary communication and interaction environment that allows remotely located visitors to interact with each other in a shared virtual environment. Visitors can integrate themselves into a three-dimensional complex virtual world of artificial life organisms that react to their body movement, motion and gestures. These artificial beings also communicate with each other as well as with part of an artificial universe, where real and artificial life are closely interrelated through interaction and exchange.
>
> (Sommerer and Mignonneau 1998: 157)

Although *Life Spaces* worked on similar principles to the artists' previous pieces, it created an even more complex interplay of the virtual and the real. The piece extended participation to online visitors who could contribute to the installation from anywhere in the world simply by sending an email message through the *Life Spaces* website. Each message initiated a creature and a corresponding sound: the more complex the message, the more complex the creature. However, the creature's design was not only the result of the initial text-message, but the consequence of its own evolutionary process, which also depended upon the interaction with the viewers of the actual environment at the ICC-NTT Museum in Tokyo, which had commissioned the work (Sommerer and Mignonneau 1998: 157). So the creatures' evolution was the result of a complex series of operations:

> [o]nce a text has been created and sent by an on-line user, a creature starts to live and interact with other creatures in the physical space of the *Life Spaces* environment at the ICC-NTT Museum in Tokyo. Not only do creatures there interact with each other, but on-site users can interact with the creatures as well by touching them, cloning them or helping them mate with each other. A special interaction set-up, similar to a virtual set, is used (for example, for

chromakeying of real actors into 3D virtual worlds) and on-
site users can find themselves displayed three-dimensionally
among the *Life Spaces* creatures.

(Sommerer and Mignonneau 2001: 304)

The virtual creatures may exhibit curiosity and fear, and may even be
killed if a viewer steps on them. Apart from the possibility of being
borne out of a viewer's design, these virtual creatures are able to
'clone' and so produce creatures with the same email text as the parent
creature. They are also able to 'reproduce' and hence give life to
creatures with an email text comprising the original email texts
of both parent creatures (Sommerer and Mignonneau 2000).

The piece lasted one year, and gave the artists the opportunity to see
how the system evolved over time. Here, as in previous works, the
viewer was directly responsible not only for the creation but for the
development of the work of art. Again, the viewer doubled their presence by being able to see themself both in the real and in the virtual
environment. Here they could interact with both the virtual creatures
and other real viewers, thus creating a microcosm defined by the
dialectic tension *between* the real and the virtual. Moreover, inside the
virtual environment an independent A-Life 'living system' was created
(*ibid.*). This could survive beyond the time of the interaction and was
even able to create offspring bearing traces of the original viewer–
creator. Here, text, information, was transformed into A-Life. Hence,
these A-Lifeforms, just like the lifeforms they emulated, were the
products of codes of information, texts of life. Thus, in *Life Spaces*, not
only was the medium the message; the message was also the medium.

Likewise, Sommerer and Mignonneau's *Verbarium* (1999) was
described as 'an interactive text-to-form editor on the Internet'
(Sommerer and Mignonneau in Weibel and Druckrey 2001: 226).
Users here were able to write text messages that could function as a
'genetic code' for the creation of a visual three-dimensional form. As
in Sommerer and Mignonneau's description, '[d]epending on the
composition of the text, the form can either be simple or complex,
or abstract or organic. All text messages together are used to build a
collective and complex three-dimensional image. This image is like a
virtual herbarium' (*ibid.*) Not only did the organisms created by information provided by the viewers come to life, but they were able to
organise themselves into a 'superior' lifeform, a metatext that was
formed by and yet superseded the original, individual text messages.
Here, as in previous works, organisms were created from hypertextualities that transcended their creators and were thus able to produce

other organisms in a seemingly independent micro-ecological system. Just as plants, animals and perhaps even human beings are being cloned from genetic codes in the real world, in the art world of Sommerer and Mignonneau, A-Life, which in itself is a form of coded text, derives from the viewers' email texts. So text here is not only meta-textual, intertextual and hypertextual, but *life* itself. And yet this process or transformation of text into life both excludes the viewer (in that, as a creator, the viewer is the author of the A-Life-originating text) and includes them (because viewers are always also genetic data, able to interact with other data, in a world in which at the end there is nothing but en-'acted' text).

Transgenetic art: the case of Eduardo Kac

The Brazilian artist Eduardo Kac, a pioneer of holopoetry, telepresence and biotelematic art, has worked with a variety of media including performance art, graffiti, fax art, digital poetry, telerobotics and transgenetic art. In 1983, Kac coined the word 'holopoetry' when creating what he described as an 'immaterial and mobile architecture of words' (Bureaud in Kostić and Dobrila 2000: 7). This work on spatialisation led him to experiment with telepresence, through which, since 1986, he has been exploring the coexistence of the human, the animal and the machine. He defines 'telepresence' as a 'union of telematics and remote physical action' that allows for the creation of artworks in which 'immediate perceptual encounters are expanded by a heightened awareness of what is absent, remote' (Kac in Goldberg 2000: 181–2). Telematic art has a 'desire to convert electronic space from a medium of representation to a medium for remote agency', so that 'actions carried out by Internet participants have direct physical manifestation in a remote gallery space' (Kac 2002). Telepresence art therefore shows that, from a social, political and philosophical point of view, what cannot be seen is equally relevant to what meets the eye (Kac in Goldberg 2000: 182).

Since 1994, Kac has also been experimenting with biotelematic art, aiming to produce a hybrid of the living and the telematic. This, after 1998, matured into an engagement with transgenetic art, which Kac describes as a form in which 'the animate and the technological can no longer be distinguished' (Kac 2002). In fact, transgenetic art aims to use genetic engineering techniques 'to transfer synthetic genes to an organism or to transfer natural genetic material from one species into another, to create unique living beings' (Kac in Stocker and Schöpf 1999: 289). Kac's work, always challenging and interrogating the boundaries of what it means to be organic, human or machinic, undoubtedly confronts complex, difficult issues concerning identity, agency, genetics, ethics, their interaction and the very 'possibility of communication' (Kac 2002) between these species. Whether by exploring the possibilities of telepresence and the biotelematic or by developing life in transgenetic art, Kac's work has illuminated and broken the far too comfortable ground upon which the human subject constructs its own identity.

At the heart of Kac's *Ornitorrinco* is the distortion of human perception produced by the machine. This piece consists of a series of works experimenting with telepresence that were developed between 1989 and 1996 in collaboration with Ed Bennett. 'Ornitorrinco' is 'platypus' in Portuguese, and was chosen because the platypus is seen as a hybrid of bird and mammal (Kac 2002). Kac suggests, 'I propose to unite three areas of aesthetic investigation that so far have been explored as separate artistic realms: robotics, telecommunications and interactivity' (*ibid.*). Thus 'Ornitorrinco in Eden' (1994) took place between Seattle, Chicago and Lexington, which represented three points of active participation, although there were also a number of points of observation. The point of view of Ornitorrinco, as experienced by the viewers, was guided in real time by viewers in Lexington and Seattle. So, '[t]he remote participants shared the body of Ornitorrinco simultaneously' (*ibid.*) and the animal represented the human point of view as perceived from two separate locations. The robot Ornitorrinco was in fact controlled via telephone or the Net, and thereby became 'a substitute-body shared and "inhabited" by the participating public' (Bureaud in Kostić and Dobrila 2000: 8). Kac suggests that the objective 'was to imply kinship between the organic (animal) and the inorganic (telerobot)' (Kac 2002), and, via telepresence, 'to metaphorically ask the viewer to look at the world from someone else's point of view. It's a nonmetaphysical out-of-body experience' (Kac in Wilson 2002: 535). Thus,

> Ornitorrinco in Eden creates a context in which anonymous participants perceive that it is only through their shared experience and non-hierarchical collaboration that little by little, or almost frame by frame, a new reality is constructed. In this new reality, spatiotemporal distances become irrelevant, virtual and real spaces become equivalent, and linguistic barriers may be temporarily removed in favour of a common empowering experience.
>
> (Kac 2002)

A subsequent piece also allowed for an exploration of the interaction between the human, the animal and the machine. *Essay Concerning Human Understanding* (1994), the result of Kac's collaboration with Ikuo Nakamura, facilitated communication between a canary in Kentucky and a philodendron plant in New York. The audience here interacted with both the plant and the bird, so the piece could be described as an environment in which 'multiple agents interacted with each other' (Shanken in Kostić and Dobrila 2000: 20). As Kac noted:

> [b]y enabling an isolated and caged animal to have a telematic conversation with a member of another species, [the] installation dramatized the role of telecommunications in our lives. The inter-species communicative experience observed in the gallery reflects our own longing for interaction, our desire to reach out and stay in touch.
>
> (Kac 2002)

Essay Concerning Human Understanding subverted a treatise by John Locke of the same title which affirmed the predominance of humankind over all other beings (Shanken in Kostić and Dobrila 2000: 20). No longer able to hold a unifying point of view, the viewer was dispersed and became just another player in this 'dramatisation' of communication.

Kac's next piece, *Teleporting an Unknown State* (1996), was a biotelematic interactive installation in which the viewer could witness the growth of a living organism through the Net. Kac, who suggests that '[t]he installation creates the experience of the Internet as a life-supporting system', describes the piece as follows: '[i]n a very dark room a pedestal with earth serves as a nursery for a single seed. Through a video projector suspended above and facing the pedestal, remote individuals send light via the Internet to enable this seed to photo-synthesise and grow in total darkness' (Kac 1998: 9). In a second version of the experiment, participants were asked to point the web cameras to the sky and teleport light directly to the plant (Kostić in Kostić and Dobrila 2000: 41). The result was that the seed planted at the beginning of the exhibition became an eighteen-inch-tall plant, and the participants had shared the responsibility that ensured the plant had grown for the duration of the installation (Kac 1998: 9). Thus, in *Teleporting an Unknown State* communication allowed for the growth of a living organism. Here, 'Internet video-conferencing is used to teleport light particles from several countries with the sole purpose of enabling biological (and not artificial) life and growth in the installation site' (Kac 2002). Kac felt that

> a new sense of community and collective responsibility emerges out of this context without the exchange of a single verbal message. Through the collaborative action of anonymous individuals around the world, photons from distant countries and cities are teleported into the gallery and are used to give birth to a fragile and small plant. It is the participants' shared responsibility that ensures that the plant grows as long as the show is open.
>
> (Kac 2002)

In *Rara Avis* (1996), Kac's experimentation with telepresence became even more complex. Here, a telerobotic bird-machine was enclosed in a gallery aviary with real birds. Spectators could assume the perspective of the bird-machine by using the Internet or data glasses, and observe themselves, or the real birds in the aviary, from the bird-machine's point of view (Stocker in Kostić and Dobrila 2000: 82). The piece, which was an interactive networked telepresence installation, also, through the Internet, allowed remote viewers to experience the gallery from the point of view of the bird as activated locally by each viewer. Remote viewers could also use their own microphones to trigger the bird's vocal apparatus, hence affecting the other birds in the aviary and subsequently probably also the viewers in the room. So, 'Network ecology and local ecology mutually affected one another' (Kac in Goldberg 2000: 187). Here, 'the identity of the viewer and its position is trapped in an endless loop involving inside and outside, freedom and captivity, seeing and being seen, to manipulate and to be manipulated', in that, '[f]rom an epistemological point of view, telerobotic technology places the viewer both inside and outside the cage' (Kusahara in Kac 2002). Thus, in *Rara Avis*, it is no longer possible to distinguish between real and virtual because the viewer's point of view is ultimately a construction of the interaction between the real and the virtual.

For *Time Capsule* (1997), Kac inserted a microchip with a programmed identification number subcutaneously into his left leg.

> At the event Kac placed his leg into a scanning apparatus, and his ankle was then webscanned from Chicago (the scanner's button was pushed via a telerobotic finger). Kac subsequently

registered himself in a Web-based animal identification database, originally designed for the recovery of lost animals.

(Paul in Kostić and Dobrila 2000: 28)

Kac defines the piece as

a work-experience that lies somewhere between a local event-installation, a site-specific work in which the site itself is both my body and a remote database, and a simulcast on TV and the Web [. . .] The temporal scale of the work is stretched between the ephemeral and the permanent; i.e., between the few minutes necessary for the completion of the basic procedure, the microchip implantation, and the permanent character of the implant.

(Kac 2002)

Not only does the implant create a reference to the fact that the ankle has traditionally been a part of the body that has been chained or branded (Beckmann 1998: 5), but 'the presence of the chip (with its recorded retrievable data) inside the body forces us to consider the co-presence of lived memories and artificial memories within us' (Kac 2002). Again, as in previous works, Kac dislodges the human as outsider to the virtual and shows how the human subject is in fact always already enmeshed in the virtual.

Similar dynamics were explored in *A-Positive* (1997). Developed with Ed Bennett and described as a 'biobotic work' (*ibid.*), *A-Positive* comprised an 'exchange of blood between a human and a robot' (Bureaud in Kostić and Dobrila 2000: 8). While the robot received human blood and extracted enough oxygen from it to keep alight a small flame, the biobot donated dextrose to the human, who accepted it intravenously. The intention was to probe 'the delicate relationship between the human body and emerging new breeds of hybrid machines that incorporate biological elements and from these elements extract sensorial and metabolic functions' and therefore show that '[n]ot even DNA or blood are immune to the invasion of the body by technology' (Kac 2002).

Subsequently, Kac developed *Genesis* (1998–2004), a transgenetic artwork that explored 'the intricate relationship between biology, belief systems, information technology, dialogical interaction, ethics and the Internet' (Kac in Ascott 2000: 17). Here,

a synthetic gene crafted by the artist and embodied by bacteria encodes a passage from the Bible. The gene mutates live through the Internet as Web participants activate a source of ultraviolet light in the gallery, thus changing the original meaning of the text.

(Stocker in Kostić and Dobrila 2000: 82)

For *Genesis*, Kac converted into Morse code the following sentence from Genesis: 'Let man have dominion over the fish of the sea and over the fowl of the air and over every living thing that moves upon the earth.' He then applied a conversion principle by which a dash became T (Thiamine), a dot became C (Cytosine), a word space became A (Adenine) and a letter space became G (Guanine). 'By chaining together, these chemical bases make up the rungs of the DNA molecule, the double-helix whose sequences of letters–genes serve as both blueprint and material for the creation of life' (Tomasula in Kostić and Dobrila 2000: 85). So, such sequences as AGC | GCT | ACC formed particular amino acids and each DNA molecule was 'both material and message, both the book and its content' (*ibid*.: 86). This new 'art gene' (*ibid*.) was then combined with a protein that could glow when illuminated by ultraviolet light, and both the protein and the gene were inserted into an E.coli species that was placed in a Petri dish, together with another strain of E.coli that was not carrying the Genesis gene, but which glowed yellow under an ultraviolet lamp. As in Sommerer and Mignonneau's work, the fluidity between text and life is determined here directly by the viewer, who is ultimately not only the creator of the work of art, but the creator of life itself. Both a maker and an onlooker of the theatre of life, the viewer's actions carry the highest ethical consequences in that they are able to change both the text of life *and* life itself. In Kac's uncomfortable work, the viewer's remote actions affect the life in the Petri dish, thus showing that the relation of real and virtual is fluid and the performance of life takes place both inside and outside the human subject.

Experimentation with transgenetic art has taken a step further in Kac's next piece, *GFP Bunny* (2000). 'My transgenetic artwork "GFP Bunny" comprises the creation of a green fluorescent rabbit (named *Alba*), its social integration, and its ensuing public debate. GFP stands for green fluorescent protein' (Kac in Kostić and Dobrila 2000: 101). The piece entailed not only the creation of the fluorescent rabbit but its exhibition as art. *GFP Bunny* is both the rabbit and the public debate, both the creation of life and the intertextuality and metatextuality deriving from it. It was designed to stimulate a debate on the notions of 'normalcy, heterogeneity, purity, hybridity and

Figure 9 GFP Bunny, Eduardo Kac and Alba. Photographer: Christelle Fontaine.

otherness', while also showing 'consideration for a non-semiotic notion of communication as the sharing of genetic material across cognitive life of transgenetic animals' (Kac in Kostić and Dobrila 2000: 102). This was intended to generate 'public respect and appreciation for the emotional and cognitive life of transgenetic animals', while also offering an 'expansion of the present practical and conceptual boundaries of artmaking to incorporate life invention' (*ibid.*).

GFP Bunny is a complex and multi-layered piece. The green fluorescent protein itself is isolated from a Pacific Northwest jelly-fish which emits a bright green light when exposed to UV or blue light (Kac in Stocker and Schöpf 1999: 289). Alba constitutes a new species because the jellyfish gene was inserted into her. So, although she is completely white, she glows when illuminated in a certain light (Kac in Kostić and Dobrila 2000: 102). Kac transformed the exhibition space in Avignon, where the piece was meant to take place, into a 'cozy living room' that included a couch where Kac himself could live with Alba for a week in order to convey the idea 'that biotechnologies are on their way to entering our lives at the most basic level: in our private homes' (Andrews in Kac 2002). At the last minute, however, the director of the institute that had created Alba refused to release her for the exhibition and the piece has sub-sequently mainly consisted of Kac's appeals to the institute for Alba's discharge.

Whatever the ethical judgement on *GFP Bunny*, the piece is clearly a pioneering work. The 'performance' of *GFP Bunny* includes a conventional gallery installation, comprising the showing of the rabbit, as well as the human subject – Kac himself – caring for it, but also the very creation of the rabbit, as well as the heated public debate on the ethics of its creation and, more unexpectedly, the insti-tute director's refusal to release it. With the creation of Alba, life turned into artwork, and its creation and existence have become a performance.

Kac's artwork has been exploring the integration of virtual and real spaces, as well as hybridity and the possibility of 'a new ecology where organic and technological systems cross-pollinate' (Bureaud in Kostić and Dobrila 2000: 8). He believes that

> [i]n the future we will have foreign genetic material in us as today we have mechanical and electronic implants. In other words, we will be transgenetic. As the concept of species based on breeding barriers is undone through genetic engin-eering, the very notion of what it means to be human is at stake. However, this does not constitute an ontological crisis. To be human will mean that the human genome is not a limitation, but our starting point.
>
> (Kac in Stocker and Schöpf 1999: 293)

By experimenting with the intersections of the real and the virtual, Kac has shown that the viewer is continually enmeshed in both, and that actions carried out in the virtual may affect the real and vice versa. Kac's viewer is dispersed and often exists only in a condition of mediation. In his work, individuality gives way to multiplicity and the real is always available only as an unstable and 'flickering' (Hayles in Druckrey 1996: 259–79) overlay of real and virtual, organic and machinic, human and animal. In his transgenetic art, Kac has also been showing that not only is the human already a cyborg, but that it is also already post-human, and that the very notion of the human is already a hybrid, not only by means of evolution, but medically, via genetic engineering. In Kac's work, this hybrid, post-human viewer, residing at the point of intersection between the real and the virtual, continuously re-enacts the uncomfortable but exciting performance of life.

Moo and Mud theatre

In 1980, two English programmers at the University of Essex, Roy Trubshaw and Richard Bartle, constructed an adventure game that several Internet users could play at once. They called the game Multi-User Dungeon. This was the first of a number of Muds that were oriented towards game-playing and puzzle-solving, whereas later ones, known as Moos or Object-Oriented Muds, allowed users to build textual objects and create landscapes. Muds and Moos are among the most popular forms of virtual environments. Users, or players, create characters, define online personae, experiment with identity, interact with one another, explore complex simulated universes and recreate *communitas*. In the performance of everyday life, these are some of the environments in which virtuality becomes theatre.

Muds and Moos are highly structured virtual spaces in which the player is able to move with a certain degree of freedom. Upon entering any such environment, the player often encounters a verbal diagram of the neighbourhood or maps of existing towns. In this way, they are familiarised with the new environment and are able to move around. In Muds, one of the main activities is the issuing of commands that move the player in space. Some environments even have modes of public transportation, such as trains, taxis or boats. Once the player is able to move and has become part of the new community, they may build their own rooms and buildings, hence adding to the 'architectural' dimension of the game.

As in hypertext practice, in Muds, players are simultaneously reading and writing, acting both as viewers and creators of these complex environments. Peter Anders describes how a New Jersey Institute of Technology School of Architecture's experiment in mapping text-based Muds showed that their structures are very complex and curiously resemble 'extremely large molecular models' which are often mapped absurdly in relation to their geographical parameters so that, for instance, a room in DreaMoo described as being west of another is accessible by going east from that room (Anders in Beckmann 1998: 222). In fact, '[m]otion in a MUD is an illusion created by the text sequence' (*ibid*.: 228). Within these virtual environments, however far the travel and however sophisticated the space created, everything is simulated and nothing takes place outside the world of text. Moreover, in most Muds and Moos, objects, as well as avatars, which are animated virtual simulations that represent the player and which may or may not have a human appearance, are 'descendants of other objects' in that object-oriented programming allows replication of core modules for editing and reconfiguration so that 'the entire MUD structure is related in this curiously genetic way' (*ibid*.: 232–3). Hence the worlds of Muds and Moos, which often simulate real-life environments, also recreate real life's genetic capacity to reproduce.

In virtual environments, players act as characters and can choose whether the characters created should reflect their own personae or substantially depart from them. Therefore, players will often experiment with their gender, race and age to create characters that differ from their real-life personae. Once online, players may interact with other 'characters', create different characters and have them interact with one another. Players may also flip in and out of character and operate characters whose behaviour is more or less consistent. In some Mud environments, the player is given the role of fighter or detective and has to act in a win-or-lose situation. The opponent may be another player, a character or the programmer of the game. Muds are often based on real spaces and are modelled on fantasy adventures involving weapons, armour, money exchanges and even the killing of monsters, giants or other players. Moos, on the other hand, are more socially oriented, with the emphasis on encountering other characters and role-playing. These environments represent excellent 'laboratories for the construction of identity' (Turkle 1995: 185) and the recreation of the body social, although here it is the programmers and the players who decide the limits of society. Shelley Turkle describes an interactive computer game based on the television series *Star Trek: The Next Generation* (1988–93) which involves over a thousand players:

> [t]hey create characters who have casual and romantic sex, who fall in love and get married, who attend ritual and celebrations. 'This is more real than my real life,' says a character who turns out to be a man playing a woman who is pretending to be a man. In this game the rules of social interaction are built not received.
>
> (Turkle in Druckrey 1996: 354)

Over the years, Mud players have developed a number of real-life simulated interactions, including fake identity and even rape. One, Joan, presented herself in the mid-1980s on CompuServe as a 'neuropsychologist in her late twenties who had been crippled, disfigured, and left mute by a drunken driver' (Wertheim 1999: 238). Only after establishing the trust and friendship of a number of users, especially other women, was it revealed that Joan was 'a New York psychiatrist who was not crippled, disfigured, mute or even female. "Joan" was in fact Alex, a man "who had become obsessed with his own experiments in being treated as a female and participating in female friendships"' (*ibid.*).

This episode posed complex questions about the 'freedom' individual users have on the Net to create representations that are equal to themselves. More serious moral and ethical questions arose when 'rape' was first committed in a virtual environment. In March 1992, a character calling himself Mr Bungle and describing himself as 'an oleaginous, Bisquick-faced clown dressed in cum-stained harlequin garb and girdled with a mistletoe-and-hemlock belt whose buckle bore the inscription "KISS ME UNDER THIS, BITCH!"' (Turkle 1995: 251, original emphasis) appeared in the LambdaMoo living room, created a phantom masquerading under another player's name and raped another character. Although he was ejected from the room, the rapist was able to continue his sexual assaults until he was finally immobilised by a Moo wizard who succeeded in erasing his character from the system (*ibid.*).

In Muds, selves are constructed in interaction with the machine and the other characters encountered. As suggested by Allucquère Rosanne Stone, 'computers are arenas for social experience and dramatic interaction, a type of media more like public theatre, and their output is used for qualitative interaction, dialogue, and conversation. Inside the little box are *other people*' (Stone 1998: 16, original emphasis). Muds and Moos create not only 'a consensual hallucination' (Gibson 1993: 67), but also a stage in which different identities can be embraced so that the players' personae can be continuously dispersed and reconfigured within the game. As suggested by Turkle,

> [i]n the MUDs the projections of self are engaged in a resolutely postmodern context. There are parallel narratives in the different rooms of the MUD; one can move forward and backward in time [. . .] Authorship is not only displaced from a solitary voice, it is exploded [. . .] And the self is not only decentered but multiplied without limit.
>
> (Turkle in Druckrey 1996: 355–6)

These environments are stages on which to encounter other players *and* theatres of the self.

A well-known example of such a community is Habitat, a virtual urban space set up in an electronic environment by Lucasfilm and Quantum Computer Services in 1986. Here viewers could interact and see representations of themselves in virtual space. Defined by its creators as a 'many-player on line virtual environment' (Morningstar and Farmer in Benedikt 1993: 274), Habitat allowed people to customise their characters and move across a region, but also go through doors and passages, and enter other regions. William Mitchell describes the regions as containing functional objects, such as cash machines, bags, books, newspapers and even guns. Players could see their own representations, flattened cartoon-like figures interacting with one another as if in a 'fake' live cartoon. In building the space, Mitchell remarks, the programmers felt that they needed to create wilderness areas so that players would not be crammed together, but also interesting places to visit and objects, so that players could find things to do (Mitchell 1999: 120). Clearly, players were using the virtual environment as a social space within which to reproduce everyday social interactions with objects, as well as with other players. In time, Habitat became increasingly like 'real life'. So, because people in Habitat were allowed to carry guns, some deaths occurred, and, subsequently, a debate took place over whether people should be allowed to carry guns in virtual environments. A real-life priest then introduced a religious dimension to the game by founding the 'Order of the Holy Walnut'. Its members pledged not to carry guns.

In the end, the game designers divided the world into two parts: in town violence was prohibited. In the wilds outside of town, it was allowed. Eventually a democratic voting process was installed and a sheriff elected. Debates then ensued about the nature of Habitat laws, the proper balance between individual freedom and law and order.

(Turkle in Druckrey 1996: 363)

As the experience of a number of these games has shown, virtual environments tend to reproduce real-life social rules, so they can be evaded and recreated, in a perfected way. Virtual environments often have the tendency to attempt to reproduce real-life conditions within the virtual environment in which they operate. This makes some virtual environments curious adaptations of the virtual to the real, proving, if anything, that virtual environments can constitute excellent documentations of the passions and neuroses of the body social. The more recent Bodies©INCorporated (1996), for instance, created by the Californian artist Victoria Vesna, is an excellent example of such a phenomenon. Bodies©INCorporated is Web-based work-in-progress described as a 'mock corporate structure' in which viewers may buy shares and order digital bodies of their choice (Kac 2002). The project is written in VRML (Virtual Reality Markup Language) and is able to create a three-dimensional representation of the player's new body, which can be seen by other participants. Within Bodies©INCorporated, there are a number of spaces, such as LIMBO©INCorporated, described as 'a grey, rather non-descript zone, where information about inert bodies that have been put on hold – bodies whose owners have abandoned or neglected them – is accessed' (*ibid.*); NECROPOLIS©INCorporated, 'a richly textured, baroque atmosphere, where owners can either look at or choose how they wish their bodies to die' (*ibid.*); and SHOWPLACE!!!©INCorporated, 'where members can participate in discussion forums, view star/featured bodies of the week, bet in the deadpools, and enter "dead" or "alive" chat sessions' (*ibid.*). Here, viewers 'become emotionally attached to their avatars and projected idealized "significant" others, giving rise to new questions of identity, information storage and retrieval about physical and virtual bodies, and social interaction in cyberspace' (*ibid.*). Bodies©INCorporated can be read as an ironic comment on today's global world, in which genetic engineering and cloning are about to change what we all can be.

As Mitchell shows, '[t]he Net negates geometry [. . .] you do not go *to* it; you log *in* from wherever you physically happen to be' (Mitchell 1999: 8–9, original emphases). The Net is not an environment separate from us; we are already in the Net. And the Net is already within us. It belongs to the very fabric of the environment of which we also are a part. The Net is a world within which 'the self is reconstituted as a fluid and polymorphous entity. Identities can be selected or discarded almost at will, as in a game or fiction' (Robins 1996: 88). Within the Net, the self is in its own fiction, suspended between the real and the virtual, transcending its physicality, striving to become other.

4

PERFORMING THROUGH THE HYPERSURFACE

The hypersurface is where the real and the virtual meet each other. It is materiality and textuality, real and representation. It is also the site of virtual performance. Through the hypersurface, the viewer can enter the work of art, be part of it, as well as interact with it. Because the hypersurface is a liminal space, the viewer can *double* their presence and be in both the real and the virtual environment simultaneously. In other words, the viewer may be part of both the realm of the image and the sphere of the real, and may modify one through the other. In performing through the hypersurface, the viewer enters the world of simulation while maintaining a direct rapport with their own environment. The theatre of the hypersurface is not immersive but it simulates immersiveness. As the multiplicity of perspectives generated by the encounter of the real and the virtual becomes apparent, the viewer may experience and experiment with them – being both present in the work and *verfremdet* estranged from it. In this sense, the hypersurface is the theatre par excellence – a hyper–sur-face, a space twice removed from the 'face'; in other words, a place twice above or beyond the world of appearance.

Hypersurface theory and liquid architecture: Noh

As early as 1972, the architect Robert Venturi pointed out that Las Vegas was a completely new city, a city made of signs (Venturi 1971). As Michael Ostwald shows in his survey of the field (Ostwald in Bell and Kennedy 2000: 661), cities have increasingly been invaded by the mediatised, the virtual (Boyer 1994 and 1996), and, while they have started to resemble one another through the erasure of difference (Sudjic 1993), they have also shown a tendency towards Disneyfication (Sorkin 1992), artifice and simulation. The appearance of the screen as part of architectural design was a major step in the direction of a hybrid architecture and the reality of a media city. Famously, the Pompidou Centre in Paris (1971–9) incorporated a media screen on its façade, and such architects as Bernard Tschumi, Jean Nouvel, Jacques Herzog and Pierre de Meuron all used buildings as urban 'transmitters' (Imperiale 2000: 22), thus viewing edifices as more than mere containers and alluding to a more hybrid, diverse functionality. And while Jean Baudrillard (1988: 19–20) denounced the architectural screen as an invasion of architecture by advertising, Bart Lootsma shows that this hybridisation has in fact led to a 'contamination' of architecture 'with other media and disciplines in order to produce a new and more robust mongrel' (Lootsma in Zellner 1999: 11).

Since the latter part of the twentieth century, architecture has been experimenting with a variety of media to explore the blurring of the virtual and the real, the inside and the outside, nature and artifice. Zaha Hadid's designs and projects, for instance, show architecture and nature becoming elements of a single landscape: '[n]ature and artifice, intervention and context, urban velocity and buildings, the whole is bound or rather flows in a continuous broken or jagged line that fills all the gaps, all the possible spaces *between* objects.' (Palumbo 2000: 43, original emphasis).

Whereas in the work of performance artists such as Stelarc the body becomes architecture, the container of art, with such architects as Hadid, Daniel Libeskind and Frank O. Gehry, architecture tends towards the organic, the biological, the *live*. No longer merely a container of people or art, architecture presents the virtual and the real, the organic and inorganic, inside and outside, as in dialogue with one another, or even as part of one another. As Maria Luisa Palumbo suggests,

> [o]ur horizon is characterised by a paradigmatic reversal of perspective. While the body, invaded and dilated by tech- nology becomes architecture, architecture in turn looks to the body, not as a model of order and formal measurement, but as a model of sensitivity, flexibility, intelligence and communicative capacity.
>
> (Palumbo 2000: 80)

As early as 1968, Coop Himmelb(l)au had stated: '[o]ur architecture has not a physical plan, but a psychic one. Walls no longer exist [. . .] Our heartbeat becomes space; our face is the façade' (Himmelb(l)au in Gerbel and Weibel 1994: 58). In rendering architecture more organic, architects such as Himmelb(l)au, as well as Hadid and Rem Koolhaas, problematised the very relationship between building and ground, the inside and the outside, functionality and use. So Palumbo points out that in this new form of architecture, 'the building refuses to take root, it rebels against the laws of gravity, it collapses and breaks up, recomposes into precarious equilibriums, in a form ready to change again, centreless, without an axis perpendicular to the ground or an evident order between the parts' (Palumbo 2000: 52).

One of the artists who has attempted to liberate architecture from Cartesian space and Euclidean form is Peter Eisenman, whose Library in Place des Nations, Geneva (1996), for instance, has a diagrammatic structure which follows the operations of human neurological activity (Galofaro 1999: 32). Likewise, in his virtual house (1987–97), created 'from the interaction of nine cubes constituting a potential field of vectorial relationships' (*ibid.*: 60), the light penetrates through the folds, and new spaces, one inside another, become possible. For this work, Eisenman was inspired by Gilles Deleuze's analysis of the fold, which was theorised as an 'in-betweenness of spaces', able to represent dialectical opposites, such as organic and inorganic, inside and outside (Deleuze 1993: 13). This kind of space, which can no longer be represented in a two-dimensional drawing, is virtual and, like Deleuze and Félix Guattari's rhizome, 'always in the middle, between things, interbeing, *intermezzo*' (Deleuze and Guattari 1988: 25).

Architectural engagement with the environment has also led to the construction of a number of ecological buildings, such as the VPRO Head Office in Hilversum, Holland (1997), built by MVRDV, which maximises the dialogue between the inside and the outside of the building by blurring the distinction between the interior and the exterior through an open-plan floor and the use of voids. Likewise, MVRDV's RVU building in Hilversum (also 1997), on the same campus as the VPRO Head Office, is intended to give the appearance of a site 'on which nothing has been built', so that '[t]he building seems to sprout from the ground, as if it were a part of the earth, or as if the topography had decided to unearth it and reveal the glazed front façade as a wound, a cut or an interruption' (Cuito 2000: 20). A similar engagement with the environment was explored by Toyo Ito's Wind Tower (1986) in Yokohama, which is 'both natural and artificial' (Prestinenza Puglisi 1999: 23) in that the tower filters the air and noises of the city and transforms them into light. Ito's engagement with media also emerged in his proposed entry for the Japanese Maison de la Culture in Paris (1992), which was titled 'Media ships sailing on the Seine' (Gerbel and Weibel 1994:33). The design was based 'on the idea of a spaceship which arrives at the Seine from Tokyo carrying information and culture'. Here, images could be projected on to the glass façade and the building's floors and walls were also a 'screen' offering information, thus giving the impression of a building in which 'spaces are created through information and are themselves temporary' (ibid.: 33–4).

Buildings will soon be 'aware' of their own alterations (Palumbo 2000: 66), and therefore will have become to some extent 'self-conscious'. For example, a house that is 'sensitive to human presence, capable of following a person's movements through the various rooms and automatically controlling the opening and closing of doors, windows, lighting and heating' has already been constructed in Sondrio, Italy, as part of the 'Progetto Facile' ('Easy Project'), in collaboration with Milan Polytechnic (ibid.: 67). Buildings of this kind are not only simulating the organic, but becoming organic, so that

> [o]ne will become aware of the fact that they [buildings] simulate the skin's functions, and artificial and sensory and motoric nerves, and will probably, sometime in the future, even build a central nervous system into them. And even further into the future one may perhaps inhabit artificial living beings.
>
> (Gerbel and Weibel 1994: 17)

To explore the complexity of this merging of real and virtual in architectural practices, the architect Stephen Perrella elaborated on the concept and practice of the hypersurface. These overlays of real and virtual 'appear in architecture where the co-presence of both material and image upon an architectural surface/membrane/substrate is such that neither the materiality nor the image dominates the problematic' (Perrella 1998: 13). In this sense, '[t]he term hyper-surface is not a concept that contains meaning, but is an event; one with a material dimension' (ibid.: 10). The hypersurface is therefore more than just a surface: it is a representation as well as a materiality. It belongs to both the world of the image and the real. Furthermore, it implies their continuous relationship one with the other. As pointed out by Marcos Novak, hypersurface is 'an effort to see surface not as an Aristotelian delimiter of space but as the portal between worlds through which subjectivity emerges' (Novak in Perrella 1998: 88). Subsequently, a hypersurface is also a surface with excess, a surface with a meta-dimension, as Perella notes,

[h]ypersurface is a reconsideration of often dichotomous relationships existing in the environment. These binaries include:
image/form, inside/outside, structure/ornament, ground/
edifice and so forth; not as separate and hence static entities
but as transversally-constituted fabrics or planes of im-
manence. Hypersurfaces are generated in the problematic
relationships that occur when binary categories conjugate
because such divisions can no longer be sustained in isolation
through either linguistic or material divisions.

(Perrella 1998: 8)

Hypersurfaces are places of exchange, fleeting intertextual strata in
which dialectical opposites interact and continuously contaminate one
another. As part of the real, they are bound to materiality: as image,
film or photography, they are both intertextual and metatextual, and
belong to the sphere of discourse. So the hypersurface 'is a zone of
exchange between consciousness (language or text) and levels of the
inorganic' (Perrella 1999: 6). Able to present dichotomous relationships, between representation and matter, inside and outside, organic
and inorganic, the hypersurface is the site of virtual performance.

Hypersurfaces are often found in innovative and experimental
forms of virtual architecture, such as what (following Novak's neo-
logism) is now known as 'liquid' architecture. Novak described this
as follows:

an architecture that breathes, pulses, leaps as one form and
lands as another. Liquid architecture is an architecture whose
form is contingent on the interests of the beholder; it is an
architecture that opens to welcome me and closes to defend
me; it is an architecture without doors and hallways, where
the next room is always where I need it to be and what I
need it to be.

(Novak in Benedikt 1993: 250)

Liquid architecture is mediated architecture that changes according to
its environment, 'a liquidising of everything that has traditionally been
crystalline and solid in architecture. It is the contamination of media'
(Spuybroek in Perrella 1998: 50). Moreover, in liquid architecture,
'[t]he design does not distinguish architecture and information as
separate entities, nor as separate disciplines' (ibid.: 51). It is therefore
information architecture, and may be inhabited and read at the same
time. A work of liquid architecture 'is no longer a single edifice, but

a continuum of edifices, smoothly or rhythmically evolving in both space and time. Judgements of a building's *performance* become akin to the evaluation of dance and theater' (Novak in Benedikt 1993: 251, original emphasis). Liquid architecture is therefore a fluid and hybrid form that is created via mediation, exists in its relationship with the environment and is seen in the process of its transformation. In this sense, it is architecture in performance, and what we witness within it is a form of theatre.

Liquid architecture was the aesthetic behind one of the most compelling buildings constructed in recent years, at Waterland in Neeltje Jans, Holland. The building consists of FreshH2O EXPO built by Lars Spuybroek and the Salt Water Pavilion built by Kas Oosterhuis from Nox (1994–7). Ineke Schwartz describes their Water Pavilion as a building in which form and content are intimately related and in which 'nothing would be predictable, no section would be the same and no angle would be square' (Schwartz 1997). 'Inside the building walking is like falling; the floors are not horizontal, and there is no reference to the horizon' (Cuito 2000: 26). The building comprises two interlocking sections, with Spuybroek's Fresh Water Pavilion leading into Oosterhuis's smaller Salt Water Pavilion.

The main entrance leads into the Fresh Water Pavilion, in which there is no distinction between horizontal and vertical, between floors, walls and ceilings. Here, the building and the exhibition have fused: a simulated geyser erupts, water splatters, projections fall directly on to the building and its visitors, the air is filled with waves of electronic sound (Schwartz 1997). Architecture and media are so 'fused' (*ibid.*) that even the very act of walking triggers sensors that convert the visitors' movements into waves of virtual water, so that every time a visitor walks through the infrared light beams, waves are projected on to the grids surrounding them. Through other sensors, light and sound are activated so that the entirety of the building becomes animate, *alive*. As suggested by Spuybroek, the Fresh Water Pavilion tries to merge hardware, software and wetware (Spuybroek in Perrella 1998: 50). Its shape is dictated by the fluid deformation of fourteen ellipses spaced out over the length of most of the building. The curves are bent and twisted by natural elements, such as the wind and the water, and the building has no horizontality and no windows. In it, the 'vertigo of the motor system is inextricably linked to sensory hallucination' (*ibid.*: 51).

In the Salt Water Pavilion, the viewer is in a space in which water drips from the walls and flows over the floor, so they experience the tidal movements of the sea to the extent of becoming trapped on one

Figure 10 Interior of FreshH20 EXPO (Fresh Water Pavilion), 1997, The Netherlands, Nox Architects.

side of the environment by the rising water levels. The lights reflect on the wet wall surfaces and images of different perceptions of water and fluidity are projected on to the walls. Through the projections, the building becomes a hypersurface. The Salt Water Pavilion is also in an open relationship with its environment because the building 'captures raw data from a weather station on a buoy in the sea, and transcribes the data into an emotional factor' (Burry 2001: 150). The building is therefore 'suddenly and simultaneously a hundred different things: a stranded whale, a late brancusi, a paramecium, a sea cucumber, a submarine, a lemniscate, a speedboat, a tadpole (with silver tail), a solidified droplet, A WAVE, A STEALTH' (Oosterhuis and Lénárd 1998; original emphasis).

In the Water Pavilion, '[f]orm and information are never separate. Form defines information and information defines form, but in doing so they adapt themselves structurally and refine themselves' (Spuybroek in Mulder and Post 2000: 123). This building is therefore not only a perfect example of liquid architecture's 'contamination by media' (Spuybroek in V2 1997: 155), but an example of its performative nature. As the spectator enters the building, it starts to perform both for and with the viewer. In a way, the building appropriates the viewer and the environment's data and therefore *becomes* the environment, and *embodies* the viewer. Here, the building, the viewer(s) and the environment are inextricably linked through the world of information. As Spuybroek suggests,

> [l]iquid architecture is always about trying to connect one act to another, about putting a virus in the program itself, about the hyperbolic linking of events, where every object and every event can have unforeseen and unprogrammed effects. Nothing, no function, no object can remain isolated; everything is involved in a continual process of transformation into the other – everything is necessarily opened up and leaking away.
>
> (Spuybroek in V2 1997: 155–9)

In the Water Pavilion, '[b]y fusing floor and wall, floor and screen, surface and interface, a plastic, liquid, and haptic architecture is achieved' (Cuito 2000: 26). In this complex hypersurface, the viewers themselves become part of both its mediatised and its material world. In fact, the viewers both constitute the information utilised by the building which is transformed into projection, into image, and represent its very materiality, the surface upon which the image is projected. Moreover, the building, which is continually changing with the visitors and the environment, actually 'displays real-time behaviour' and behaves like 'an organism at work' (Oosterhuis and Lénárd 1998). Thus the building itself continuously evolves and responds to its viewers:

> [t]he software built into the Water Pavilion receives so many different sorts of input that even the makers cannot predict the results. Every moment is different and unexpected. Which makes the Water Pavilion not just an experience but an unparalleled testing ground for the study of interactivity.
>
> (Schwartz 1997)

In Spuybroek's subsequent project for the Beechness Hotel in Noordwijk (1997), the fabric enveloping the hotel's tower was designed to be used for multiple projections, such as the faces of the hotel guests inside, seascapes, sunsets or even films (Spuybroek in Perella 1998: 35). In Beechness, the inside becomes the outside, the mediatised, the fictional and the real merge, while in the rooms (all equipped with flotation tanks) images may be projected on to the walls, creating a situation of 'polar inertia' (*ibid.*). Here, the liquidity of the architecture and the hypersurface of the façade transform the building into a theatre whose programme is continuously changing, depending on the guests inside and the programmer's editing of fact and fiction. Similarly, Oosterhuis's collaboration with Novak for TransPORTs2001 was intended to be a performing structure for ports around the world which could be manipulated on the Web by players, who would be able to modify real buildings through a real-time evolution game (Burry 2001: 188–91).

Through hypersurface theory and practice, it is possible to conceive of the surface as a skin, and therefore a site of exchange between inside and outside. Because of this, the hypersurface is also a site of potential intervention. Here, the viewer can interfere with the real through the virtual and vice versa. Within the hypersurface, the relationship between the world of information and the real is subsequently exposed. When 'performing' the hypersurface, the viewer always confronts materiality and representation, inside and outside, information and fiction, to find that they also are always part of both worlds. As a hypersurface, viewers can be both materiality and representation, both inside and outside the work of art, transformed into artistic information that changes in real time. Within the world of the hypersurface, the viewer is both remediated and in the real; they are both alive *and* live.

The game of real and virtual: the case of Paul Sermon

Since the 1970s, the sphere of telecommunications has been a rich field for artistic innovation. One of the earliest experiments with telepresence was conducted in Allan Kaprow's *Hello* (1969), a 'multi-site happening' which 'used the facilities of WGBH-TV in Boston to link four locations in the Boston area: a hospital, an educational videotape library, the Boston airport and MIT' (Saltz 2001: 73). Another early experiment with telecommunications took place in 1977 when the artist Douglas Davis created a live telecast which was transmitted via satellite to over thirty countries. This concluded with Davis's *The Last Nine Minutes*, in which the artist 'tried to break through the TV screen and reach the other performers' (Popper 1993: 137). The same year, Kit Galloway and Sherrie Rabinowitz of Mobile Image produced the *Satellite Arts Project*, in which several groups of dancers interacted with one another from different sites, creating 'a performance space with no geographic boundaries' (Galloway and Rabinowitz in Saltz 2001: 73). Three years later, the artists realised the project *Hole in Space*, which was facilitated by a satellite link between New York and Los Angeles.

Here, a number of video cameras and displays were installed in a department store in Los Angeles and the Lincoln Center in New York, 'so that the public could communicate by image and voice' (Popper 1993: 136–7). As there had been no advance publicity, and no signs or instructions for the understanding and making of the piece were available at either site, *Hole in Space* was 'simply discovered by passers-by who were suddenly confronted by images on the screen. The crowds drawn into this "hole" in space/time were able to communicate with the opposite group in the other city with less inhibition, because neither group could see itself' (*ibid.*).

Other early examples of experimentation with telecommunications are Robert Adrian X's *Die Welt in 24 Stunden* (*The World in 24 Hours*; 1982), in which artists from sixteen different cities communicated with one another and exchanged art on the Net (Baumgärtel in Weibel and Druckrey 2001: 156) and Nam June Paik's mid-1980s series of performances using a television satellite, such as *Good Morning Mr Orwell* (1984), which connected New York, Paris and New Delhi, and saw the participation of Laurie Anderson, Allen Ginsberg, Joseph Beuys and John Cage, among others. Likewise, *Bye Bye Kipling* (1987) connected New York, Seoul and Tokyo, and included such artists as Lou Reed, Keith Haring and Philip Glass, and *Wrap around the World* (1988), organised to coincide with the Olympic Games in Korea, which featured David Bowie and Merce Cunningham (Baumgärtel 2001: 37–8). All these experiments attempted to connect distant participants and thereby dealt with the creation of a new type of space that both included and superseded all actual localities from which the participants were broadcasting. This new space was constituted by the interaction of a number of real spaces through virtuality. It was a mediated, inter-local, virtual space that shared some of the characteristics of other mediated spaces, such as those developed in experiments through television, film and video art, for instance, while also moving beyond them by allowing for greater flexibility in dealing with simultaneous broadcasting from geographically remote locations. In this new space, the virtual allowed for the paradoxical and seemingly impossible overlap of different geographies of the real.

The British artist Paul Sermon has similarly experimented with teleconferencing and telematics. In *Telematic Vision* (1993), two sofas positioned in two different locations were integrated virtually through ISDN telephone links. These transmitted live chromakey-edited video images through which participants could interact telematically in the virtual space created on the monitor by moving in their own respective environments. Viewers therefore found themselves sitting on a real sofa watching a television that was broadcasting their own presence in the 'real' space. So viewers could see themselves as another would see them and were thus able to create 'their own television program by becoming the voyeurs of their own spectacle' (Sermon 2003). However, once a viewer from the other remote location sat on their sofa, the two images were merged and the first viewer could see themself sitting alongside the viewer from the remote location. Once viewers were connected on the television set, they could start to explore the possibilities of interaction offered by the virtual encounter through a joint telematic vision.

Similar dynamics were explored in Sermon's later piece *The Tables Turned* (1997), which comprised a table and a number of chairs set in two different locations. The drawers of each table contained fragments of texts and objects. One or more viewers sitting at one table could interact virtually with the viewers sitting at the other table and attempt to create a coherent narrative by putting together the fragments recomposing the last verse of William Wordsworth's ballad 'The Tables Turned' (Schwarz 1997: 146). Viewers could also just try to interact with one another by hiding parts of their own bodies in a glove or behind a mask and see how they could superimpose themselves upon the viewers in the other room. In the piece, viewers

> start to explore the space and understand they are now in complete physical control of a telepresent body that can interact with the other person. The more intimate and sophisticated the interaction becomes, the further the user enters into the telematic space. The division between the remote telepresent body and actual physical body disappears, leaving only one body that exists in and between both locations.
>
> (Sermon 2003)

In fact, the viewers' relation to their own telepresent bodies in *The Tables Turned* was almost prosthetic-like, as if the virtual body was more of an extension of the real than a representation of it. As indicated by Sermon, the better the interaction, the less aware were the viewers of their 'real' surroundings, thus, at least for a moment, allowing the viewer to exist virtually, *between* locations. Here, as in *Telematic Vision*, distant geographies could therefore be seen in a flickering moment of cohabitation.

The multiplication of locations via the use of the medium raises questions about the relationship between the virtual and the real. Paul

Virilio points out that when individuals communicate in real time through interactive techniques,

> the direct, face-to-face contact is made possible by the absolute speed of electromagnetic waves, regardless of the intervals in time and space that actually separate them. Here the event does not take 'place' or rather, *it takes place twice*. The topic aspect gives way to the teletopic aspect, the unity of time and place is split between the transmission and reception of the signals, both here and there *simultaneously*, thanks to the technical wizardry of electromagnetic inter-activity.
>
> (Virilio in V2 1997: 339, original emphases)

According to Virilio, an event occurring in a telematic encounter that is the result of the overlapping of two or more locations, as is the case in Sermon's *Telematic Vision* and *The Tables Turned*, occurs 'twice': in the real and 'simultaneously' in the virtual. This suggests that '[t]he "real" and the "represented" are being switched optically in such a way that the body of the observer is the only thing still present in his here and now and becomes the last mainstay of someone who is otherwise immersed in a virtual environment' (Virilio in V2 1997: 339–43).

The interplay of the real and the virtual is schizophrenic in nature. The observer is still physically in the 'real' and yet what they see represented is not a mere 'representation' of themselves but a technologically mediated real, a 'switched' real. In Sermon's works, the virtual and the real are therefore not only intertwined, as if engaged in the chasing game of real, virtual and mediation, but inter-dependent, the condition *sine qua non* of their mutual existence. In many ways, they are each the shadow of the other.

In an earlier piece, *Telematic Dreaming* (1992), Sermon had utilised two beds set in different locations, and had taken experimentation with telepresence further by adding a performed dimension to the piece. On one bed, in a space inaccessible to the audience, was the artist himself; on the other was the spectator. Through a camera, the bed on which the artist lay was projected onto the bed in the exhibition space so that 'a visitor can lie or sit with "the artist" on this bed and both can react to each other and make contact, at a distance' (Mulder and Post 2000: 75). Susan Kozel describes her emotions in seeing the piece as follows: '[b]y observing monitors around his bed, he [Sermon] was able to respond to the move-

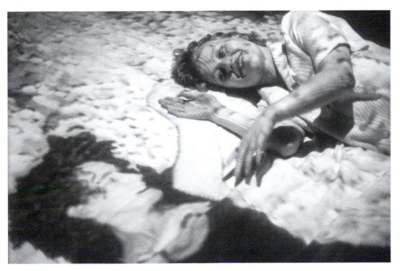

Figure 11 Telematic Dreaming, 1993, courtesy of Paul Sermon.

ments of the person. The effect was astonishing: it was one of contact improvisation between an image and a person, between ghost and matter' (Kozel 1994a: 36). Most striking is that the virtual 'presence' is reduced to a flat image and yet this image clearly leads and even directs the piece:

> [t]he intimacy between the two divergent bodies was compelling. The people tended to be shy of Paul's image on the bed. It was common for them to sit upright on the edge of the bed and tentatively reach for his hands. He responded slowly, gently, making his movements match theirs. He danced with them. It became clear that the position of power was Paul's. Paradoxically, even though he appeared as a projected image he was still able to intimidate [. . .] In his work Paul's body became virtual (i.e. a projected image), yet the rapport between image and person was very real and evoked a social and sexual dynamic familiar to us all.
>
> (Kozel 1994a: 36)

As pointed out by Sermon, *Telematic Dreaming* 'deliberately plays with the ambiguous connotations of a bed as a telepresent projection surface' (Sermon in Wilson 2002: 520). And it is precisely the context of the bed that makes the experiment more socially charged:

[t]he ability to exist outside of the user's own space and time is created by an alarmingly real sense of touch that is enhanced by the context of the bed and caused by an acute shift of senses in this telematic space [. . .] [O]nce the viewer takes on the role of the performer they lose contact with the audience and discover that the actual performance is taking place within the telematic space, and not on the bed or sofa [. . .] Bringing your self back to your actual body is as hard as getting your self onto the bed or sofa in the first place, and being able to communicate in the actual space and the telematic space simultaneously is almost impossible.

(Sermon in Wilson 2002: 520)

Interestingly, the socially charged environment of the bed seemed to intensify both the performer's and the viewer's experience of the piece. There appeared to be an absorption of the real into the virtual. The use of the medium refocused the viewer's attention so that they perceived themself as within the screen in the first instance and outside the screen only if and when distracted from the world of the screen itself. Thus, for instance, Kozel describes her experience of performing the piece as follows:

[t]he bed became my performance space. Our movement occurred in real time, but in a space which was entirely created by technology. I was alone on my bed, moving my arm and legs in physical space as if in some sort of hypnotic ritual dance, yet in virtual space I carried on intense physical improvisation with other unknown bodies.

(Kozel 1994b: 12)

Moreover, as Sermon points out, '[w]hen you move around in the bed, you actually look at a monitor, looking at your own body movement. That body is really where the effect is and where your body effect is, is really where you are' (Sermon in Anon 1994: 87). Kozel describes this experience as 'one of extending my body, not losing or substituting it' (Kozel 1994b: 13). This appropriation of the representation as a prosthetic part of one's own body explains Kozel's reactions when faced with threatening behaviour by one member of the audience who had a knife and made her feel uncomfortable, or another who elbowed her in the stomach and made her feel physically shaken, or, even more brutally, when two members of the audience literally assaulted her virtual image, an incident so horrific that Kozel detached herself from her virtual persona in what she describes as 'an involuntary act of self preservation – a primordial reaction in a sophisticated technological context' (*ibid.*: 13).

In *Telematic Dreaming*, the virtual became both a medium through which to see the real – the spectacle of the real – and a mediated 'extension' of the real that allowed the encounter between performers and viewers whose real bodies were located in different spaces. In this instance, the virtual was able to capture the viewer's gaze and, like a parasite, refocus their attention to such an extent that both artists who practised the piece describe difficulty in getting back to the unmediated world of their own 'real' bodies. At the same time, the performance space was also transformed into a hypersurface, combining the real bed and the mediated moving image of the performer, and thus creating, despite the non-immersive quality of the piece, enough of a lifelike hallucination to lure the viewer into entering a communication with the realm of the image as if 'real'. Through the hypersurface the image of the performer thus became the *live* performer, and so paradoxically the virtual became 'real' again.

All simulated: Knowbotic Research

Knowbotic Research, or KR+cF, was founded in 1991 by the Austrian artists Christian Hübler and Alexander Tuchacek and the German artist Yvonne Wilhelm. The company designs art projects in which 'information and knowledge structures are transformed into spaces of experience and agency, emphasizing process-like and non-locatable elements' (Knowbotic Research in V2 1997: 59). Knowbotic Research's artwork has focused on the processes instigated by information technology and, in later works, on the concept and practice of urbanisation. Their work primarily comprises 'investigations of the nature of information in the contemporary technology-mediated world' (Wilson 2002: 83). For them, '[i]nterfacing reality means intervene in reality' (Hübler 1997), so the company's use of the machinic 'refers not only to technical hardware, but [. . .] embraces the entire social, technical and cultural dispositive of the urban field of action' (Broekmann in V2 1997: 63). In Knowbotic Research's work 'the human and the machinic can no longer be easily distinguished' (Knowbotic Research in Wilson 2002: 387), and the idea of electronic network incorporates the human agent that is both floating inside it and operating it from outside (Hübler 1997). This revision of electronic space has induced Knowbotic Research to present the idea of the 'global' as a set of interconnecting localities while treating the urban as an overlay of both the real and the virtual. Thus, in the artwork of Knowbotic Research, 'electronic networks are not so much a global but a translocal structure which connects many local situations and creates a heterogeneous translocal stratum, rather than a homogeneous global stratum' (Knowbotic Research in V2 1998: 198).

The company's work offers 'no nice images; no trees, no buildings, no plants. They show interactivity itself. They understand that the image should deal with processing, not with representation' (Weibel in Mulder and Post 2000: 63). Its artwork problematises and to some extent even politicises the notions of presence and visibility, and there is a constant interdependency between the world of information and practised space. So participants, by altering the data flow, can influence the construction of other individuals' environments and subsequently effect their own presence and visibility within them. The interplay between the real and the virtual data flow is thus exhibited as a fluid process–oriented exchange within which the viewer may intervene in the dialectical interaction of the virtual and the real. In this simulated world, neither the machinic nor the human is entirely independent from the other, and the artwork manifests itself as the window that allows for the intervention of one world into the other. Here, '[t]he interface is not a border. It is a field of fluctuating activities' (Hübler in Mulder and Post 2000: 116).

The name of the company refers to the idea of experimentation with knowbots, 'semi–autonomous software agents that could locate, manipulate, and present information' (Wilson 2002: 838). Described as 'pure form, mathematical functions that can change themselves [and] create multiple copies of themselves' (Weibel in Hünnekens 1997: 62), knowbots are 'creatures possessing human properties such as (artificial) intelligence, (artificial) life, and (artificial) conscience, yet without any material existence'. They 'represent the subject lacking ontological status' and constitute the primary agent of a 'post–ontological art' form, but they do not have material bodies and may be both multilocal and omnipresent (Weibel in Druckrey 1996: 350). In a number of ways, they are the new 'other' to the human. They may operate *for* the human, *against* the human, and *as* and *after* the human. They belong to a post–human, all–simulated world that may be read as part of the real but also as a means to interpret it.

Interested in 'nonlinearity, multidimensionality, acceleration, compression, multiple layers, poly–perspectives, multifunctionality' (Wilson 2002: 837), Knowbotic Research claims that new technologies allow for the creation of 'non–locations' and 'mem_branes' functioning as 'zones of difference which generate confrontation and point beyond the cross-communicated indexical exchange of information' (Knowbotic Research in Wilson 2002: 837). It is through these non-locations and 'mem_branes' that individual viewers may enter the machinic and become part of a post-human rhizomatic world. Individuals are fused with the machinic and their data processed 'knowbotically' in 'global' non-locations through the World Wide Web. Here, no longer is the virtual an alternative representation of the real, but rather another way of reading the real. Following Otto Rössler's theory of endophysics, Knowbotic Research argues that the world is not so much the place where we live, but rather 'the interface through which we perceive and act' and that subsequently 'the city is not "the world of urban forces" but the interface through which we interact and negotiate with urban forces' (Knowbotic Research in V2 1998: 194). Knowbotic Research therefore shows through its work how 'post-ontological art represents a dynamic model of covariance between observer, interface, and environment, where the observer may be incorporated as part of that environment or context, constituting a dissipative structure' (Weibel in Druckrey 1996: 350). Instead of the 'conventional world of the picture' in post-ontological art, there is 'a universe of "free variables" floating in specific event-worlds, which can be comprehensively filled or replaced, and which interact with one another' (ibid.: 350–1). Consequently, the viewer is always part of the artwork, part of the mechanisms that are utilised to read the world.

An important part of the company's work has been the 'biologiza-tion of technology' (Knowbotic Research in V2 1997: 71). Knowbotic Research's art exposes the interface itself as a liminal space in which the human and the machinic, the real and the virtual, are able to cohabit. Thus, describing this moment of co-existence, they claim:

> [r]eworking the digital material and entering the formaliza-tions of the machinic in our real space/data space installations implies the temporary merging with the assemblage. The schizophrenia of that situation is very important to us: on the one hand, the merging with the situation, and on the other hand the realization that the relation between user and machine is mediated and full of tension and friction. Complete dissolution or merging, no longer knowing where I am, only makes sense if this condition alternates with phases where I am aware of this process. As one moves back and

forth in this intermediary field, as the personal appears and disappears, specific processes of subjectification, perhaps of machinic subjectifications, may be possible.

(Knowbotic Research in V2 1997: 71)

In Knowbotic Research's work, the subject is 'always in a state of becoming, defining itself in relation to new machinic contextualizations of actions which have new, particular subjectifying effects' (Knowbotic Research in V2 1997: 75). Here, the schizophrenic multiple subject is in a state of constant flux, tending towards the machinic, towards multiplicity and then yet again reconfiguring itself as the one and only human subject needed for the creation of interpretation. Here, it is the very relationship with information, with the machinic, that is problematised. The liquidity of Knowbotic Research's work produces strident tensions. This hypersurface is like a micro-universe in which the leakages and transformations that allow the interrelationship between the human and the machinic, the real and the virtual, are exposed, so that the viewer can see themself as human *and* machinic, one *and* multiple.

10_DENCIES – Questioning Urbanity (1997–9) was a long-term project that dealt with 'the possibilities of agency, collaboration and construction in translocal and networked environments' (Knowbotic Research in V2 1998: 186). The project looked at urban settings in a number of cities by analysing the 'force fields' present in particular urban situations and offering experimental interfaces that allowed for interaction with these local force fields. The aim was to 'create events through which it becomes possible to rethink urban planning and construction and arrive at a notion of process-oriented collaborative agency' (*ibid.*). The areas explored in different stages of the project were Tokyo, São Paulo and the Ruhr region of Germany, which were all analysed with different systems. In Tokyo (1997), Knowbotic Research worked in collaboration with the local architect Sota Ichikawa to identify a number of 'zones of intensity' through which certain 'qualities of urban movement (architectural, economic, human, information, traffic)' were written into a notation system (*ibid.*: 188). These movements were then digitally coded and could be observed and manipulated through the Internet. In this way, 'the non-local topology of the network and the local socio-topology of the city were meshed together via an interface' (Broeckmann in Weibel and Schmid 2000: 62). A java-based online interface allowed visitors from the terminals at the exhibition and Internet users to log in and intervene into transcoded, hypothetical processes and flows of forces that were analysed in and remapped onto the Shimbashi area in central Tokyo. These activities in the 'zone of intervention' on the Net triggered controlled light and sound effects in an installation at the exhibition site [. . .] While the agents on the Net were physically absent, yet visible through their activities, the visitors of the installation were physically visible, yet passive and absent with respect to the 'zone of intervention'.

(Broekmann in Knowbotic Research 1997: 29)

Viewers could use a number of functions which included 'conforming, opposing, drifting, confusing, repulsing, organising, deleting, merging, weakening, etc.' (Knowbotic Research in V2 1998: 188). As viewers started to interact with the environment, the program identified participants with similar interests and connected them online. Subsequently, the characters of the data movements could be changed collectively and 'in tendencies' (*ibid.*), and hereby made 'stronger, weaker, wilder, thinner, more turbulent, open, dense' (Knowbotic Research 2003). As described by Andreas Broekmann, the streams of the manipulated movements were made visible and audible in the exhibition space. Moreover, '[i]f a certain user engaged strongly in the processes of the Net, the sounds generated by his activities changed the intensity and scale of the exhibition space with dynamic changing layers of ambient noise' (*ibid.*). Yet these changes did not always indicate the actual presence of a viewer. The system could remember the past presence of a viewer and show their absence by revitalising their activities some time after the original intervention had taken place (Knowbotic Research in V2 1998: 188):

[a]n interface to the urban machine like the '10_DENCIES' project forms a 'point of discontinuity' in the city's surface, it is both a point of presence and of expression. The site of agency is both absent and present. The subject becomes 'visible' as a potential in the process of transformation. Its presence is not necessarily manifested as a physical visibility, but through the perceivability of actions.

(Broekmann in Knowbotic Research 1997: 30)

In *10_DENCIES*, Knowbotic Research transformed movement recorded from such places as railway stations, markets, hotels and similar public spaces into 'flow charts' that could be modified online

(Mulder and Post 2000: 141), thus creating a hypersurface that contained both the data of the 'real' movement of the city and the 'virtual' movement initiated by the online visitors. This flickering and continuously changing flow between the real and the virtual created through the interface of the artwork constituted the process by which the performance of *10_DENCIES* was being continuously assembled. Beyond the world of representation, *10_DENCIES* offered a window on to the real through which the viewer could continually view themself acting within it.

Knowbotic Research argues that in *10_DENCIES* it attempted 'to engage with the friction and the heterogeneity of the urban environment by merging the closed and rational system of digital computer networks with the incoherent, rhizomatic structure of the urban space' (Knowbotic Research in V2 1998: 186). In fact, in their work, the urban is constructed 'as a machinic assemblage which consists not so much of built forms and infrastructures, but of a heterogeneous field consisting of lines of forces, lines of action and interaction'. Thus, 'we see the city not as a representation of the urban forces, but as the interface to these urban forces and processes. Therefore, the city features not as a representation, but as an interface which has to be made and remade all the time' (*ibid.*: 192). So, *10_DENCIES* is a constantly variable performance of the real as seen and thereby modified through the virtual by a number of viewers working both individually and collectively. Because of this interdependence of real and virtual, '[r]ather than the submersion in a distinct and detached environment, we are trying consciously to enhance the oscillation between the fields of action of the real urban space, and those of the data space' (Knowbotic Research in V2 1997: 63). In this sense, the world of art dealt with by Knowbotic Research is both liquid and rhizomatic. It is a non-representational, non-locational, non-global, non-individual, post-human, time-oriented art in which the process of the modification of the information of the data flow is the artwork itself. It is precisely this interplay of imprecision and uncertainty in interpreting the information-bank of the real that is at the heart of the work. So,

> we are interested in finding out whether there are possibilities to approach the current changes of the urban environments through interfacing them with the data space, in order to introduce forms of doubt and resistance. We are no longer so much concerned with the processing and handling of given data, but with strategies of dealing with imprecisions

and uncertainty between experiential space and data space, between technology, perception and action.

(Knowbotic Research in V2 1997: 67)

In *10_DENCIES* Knowbotic Research transforms the capacity of the virtual to map and read the real into a vehicle for performance, so allowing the viewer to make their own perception and agency within the virtual's interplay with the real the subject of the work of art. Here the virtual is no longer just a map or representation of the real but a possibility of action. Thus, in Knowbotic Research's work, the hypersurface itself becomes the location of the spectacle through which the participant may be seen as interacting between the real and the virtual.

About war and inaction: Blast Theory's *Desert Rain*

Blast Theory's *Desert Rain* (1999–2003), devised with the Computer Research Group of the School of Computer Science at Nottingham

Figure 12 Desert Rain. 1999, interactive game, installation and performance. A collaboration with the Mixed Reality Lab, University of Nottingham. Co-commissioned by ZKM Centre for Arts and Media, Karlsruhe and Contemporary Archives, Nottingham, in association with DA2, Bristol and KTH, Stockholm. Funded by the European Commission's Kaleidoscope Fund and Arts Council England with Lottery Funds. © Blast Theory.

University, was one of the most complex and powerful responses to the first Gulf War to be produced within the sphere of theatrical practice. The piece may be seen not only as a comment on the war itself, but also as an exposure of the crucial role that technology played within both the making and the viewing of the conflict. *Desert Rain*, which has been described as a mixture of 'performance, game, installation and virtual reality' (Adams and Row Farr in Leeker 2001: 744), was inspired by Jean Baudrillard's *The Gulf War Did Not Take Place* (1991) (Clarke 2001: 44), in which the French philosopher argues that, despite the massive aerial bombardment of Iraq's military and civil infrastructure, and despite the 100,000 estimated dead, the first Gulf War did not share any of the characteristics of previous 'conventional' wars, and so, in effect, the 'war' did not take place.

Desert Rain 'attempts to articulate the ways in which the real, the virtual, the fictional and the imaginary have become increasingly entwined' (Adams in Blast Theory 2002). Throughout the piece, the viewer could encounter a series of personae, environments and phenomena that were the product of both fact and fiction, and which could be seen both in the 'real' and in the virtual environment. Moreover, *Desert Rain* carefully constructed itself as an overlay of 'real' events and simulations referring to a conflict, the first Gulf War, which was, as Baudrillard has shown, in many ways a 'mediated' war, in that it was conducted – though of course not always experienced – through the media. Thus, during the first Gulf War everything was 'performed' and much coverage was 'covered', or even completely silenced. So, 'the planes are hidden, the tanks are buried, Israel plays dead, the images are censored and all information is blockaded in the desert: only TV functions as a medium without a message' (Baudrillard 1995: 63). Reflecting this, *Desert Rain* could be conducted and experienced only through other media, and even the performers were hiding from the audience, though carefully orchestrating its every movement. By shifting from one media to another, from the real to the virtual, from the fact to the performed, *Desert Rain* attempted to destabilise the viewer's position continuously, in relation both to the practice of 'conflict' (by playing at being at war within the simulated environment of a computer game) and to that of making theatre, thus inducing the viewer into finally questioning the perceived relationship of real and virtual, as well as their own participation in and experience of the piece itself.

Desert Rain began with a performer leading six visitors into a kind of antechamber, where the audience members were asked to give up their coats and bags, and in return each received a hooded black jacket and a card with the picture of a person, their objective, who presumably had to be found. The viewer was not told whether the objective was real or fictitious, whether they were alive or dead, or even what to do once they had been found. The viewer would not even know whether the objective was ever to be encountered in the flesh, or whether they were avatars, real people or characters in someone's fiction. After this introductory moment, the audience was led through darkness into another chamber, which was divided into six cubicles, one for each viewer. Here, standing on platforms and facing a fine water spray or rain-screen upon which the virtual world was projected, they could travel through the virtual environment by moving their weight on the footpads that acted as 'large joysticks' (Blast Theory 2002). This moment marked the 'second' and virtual beginning of the piece, during which the viewers, temporarily transformed into virtual-reality players and avatars, could start to search the virtual environment for their objectives:

> [w]orking largely with computer game logic of find, retrieve, kill or rescue, the target to find is a virtual person recognizable by both name and face within the virtual environment. The goal is to find this target and escape with the other five participants to a hotel room in the virtual environment within an allotted time of 20 minutes.
>
> (Clarke 2001: 44)

After leaving the projected virtual motel room in which CNN coverage of the first Gulf War was broadcast, viewers found themselves in a desert that had been created as a projection on the virtual rain-screen (hence, presumably, the title of the piece, *Desert Rain*). Here, the viewers could meet one another through their avatars, which consisted of geometrical forms with flags representing the pictures of their objectives. The faces of these targets were 'the only figurative attributes within the abstracted linear computer-game graphics' (Clarke 2001: 44). The only known factor at this point was the fact that the targets had to be found, which raised the questions: 'what are my targets for? Am I saving them? Are they annihilated when I find them? [. . .] if they are white, what are they being targeted for?' (*ibid.*). The players did not know that they themselves were being monitored by two members of the company, who, invisibly, watched over them from behind the rain-screen and from the control room, and whose aim it was to 'support, encourage and exhort the players via an audio link' (Blast Theory 2002) so that the performance could progress smoothly. Players could therefore hear both the voices of the other 'real' players and the voice of the helper–performer, who was, of course, just another kind of player in this game of desert and rain.

The desert landscape contained three buildings. The first held a map of the environment; the second was a cylinder with six doors leading to pictures of each of the visitors on their respective platforms – an environment which therefore created a link between the virtual and the real (Adams and Row Farr in Leeker 2001: 745–6); and finally, the third building initially seemed empty but contained the viewers' targets. At this crucial moment in the piece, the virtual environment was unexpectedly penetrated by a real performer who slowly emerged through the rain-screen to hand each viewer another magnetic card. No words were spoken, and as quickly and mysteriously as the performer had appeared, they would disappear again, as if swallowed up by the world behind the screen. At this point the viewer did not know the significance of the new card, nor exactly what the consequences of finding their target had been. This moment of interruption of the virtual, of reappropriation of the virtual by the real, represented the most disturbing instance in this complex piece. So far, the viewers' only encounter with the performers had been, to some extent, functional, with the performers handing out instructions and escorting the viewers from one place to another. Viewers could therefore be mistakenly under the impression of not being in a piece of theatre at all. The spectacular *coup de théâtre*, however, brought the viewers right back from the virtual into the 'real', and from there into the world of performance, thus creating a kind of media vortex in which the various worlds explored by the piece suddenly manifested themselves to the viewer in rapid succession.

> This momentary interruption of the game disrupts the telepresence experienced by the participant, for it fractures their solipsistic virtual engagement with the screen and points to the potential of something existing beyond the realms of the image [. . .] It is therefore the performing live presence existing alongside the virtual world that enables a critique of virtual technologies to be considered.
>
> (Clarke in Blast Theory 2002)

The exchange of one card for another led to the beginning of a third phase of *Desert Rain* in which viewers found themselves in a vast underground hangar containing numbers, which were estimates of Iraqi casualties. This part of the game could be successfully completed only if all the players reached the end of the corridor. Players who had reached this phase were therefore encouraged to help others who still had to find their target.

Once the virtual-world experience was concluded, the final phase of the performance could start. Having left the virtual world in a ritual act of purification by walking through the water-screens, the viewers found that the narrow exit corridor was blocked by a large mountain of sand. Having climbed up and come down the other side, they would find that they had reached the final room of the piece. This space, simulating a motel room, contained a television that could be activated by swiping the card obtained from the performers during the virtual game. By swiping the card, each viewer's target appeared on the monitor, sitting in the same motel room that the viewers now occupied. At this point, it became manifest that each of the six targets had had their life changed by the war. The targets were: Glen, a soldier who served in the war; Shona, a soldier who was bedridden at the time of the war and watched it on television; Richard, a peace worker on the Iraqi–Saudi border; Sam, an actor who played a soldier in a television drama about the war; Eamonn, a BBC journalist who was in Baghdad when the air-raids started; and Tony, an actor who was on holiday in Egypt at the time of the conflict. All six targets had been talking about their relationship to the events during the conflict and how 'real' it all felt (Blast Theory 2000). However, even at this point it was impossible for the viewers to tell whether the targets were real or fictional, and one of the two actors even spoke about the event as 'layer upon layer of simulation reverberating from every surface' (Clarke 2001: 47). At no point did the piece therefore offer a synthesis or clarification of its structure, thus suggesting that in today's society of spectacle it is no longer possible to tell the real from the virtual.

Upon leaving the room, the viewers could finally change back into their own clothes, presumably thinking that the performance was now over. However, some time later, they would each find in their pocket a small box containing 100,000 sand grains and a quotation from General Colin Powell from the *New York Times* of 23 March 1991, in which, in reference to the possible number of Iraqis killed during the war, he said, '[i]t's really not a number I'm terribly interested in.'

Desert Rain was in many ways about 'the fragility and interconnectedness of the physical and the virtual, the fictional and the factual' (Clarke 2001: 44). The participants were taken through a journey, from the real to the virtual and then back again, only to find out that what appeared as virtual could in fact be real and hence also leave a real trace (of sand) in the viewers' lives. Likewise, what appeared to be real was mainly performed and thus, in other words, simulated.

As suggested by Rachel Clarke, 'the route feels more like a labyrinth, and disorients the body in a very corporeal way' (*ibid.*: 47). Even in the virtual environment, '[t]he participant is often floating in a void that has only compass and degree points to show the way' (*ibid.*: 45). The very set of *Desert Rain* was a combination of 'the real and the virtual, each mirroring the design of the other, and connected through the permeable and physically traversable rain curtain' (Blast Theory 2002). In this space, in which the various performance places mirrored one another, the rain-screen represented the liminal gateway linking the worlds of the image and the real. It was a hypersurface that disturbingly allowed for slippages between the two worlds: that of the cloaked performer approaching the viewer from behind the screen once the target had been found and then the viewer's own exit through the rain screen into the next phase of the performance. Here, just as in the real conflict, 'the real penetrates into the virtual and vice versa' (Adams and Row Farr in Leeker 2001: 744).

In *The Gulf War Did Not Take Place*, Baudrillard argues, '[n]o question that, in their war, the Iraqis went to war. No question that the Other came from their computers' (Baudrillard 1995: 63). So, the same event can be virtual for one set of people and real for another. Much of the war, of course, was conducted virtually, at a distance. Thus, virtual environments were incorporated into operational warplanes, 'filtering the real scene and presenting aircrew with a more readable world' (Patton in Baudrillard 1995: 4). American agents even introduced a computer virus into Iraq's air defence command and control system (*ibid.*: 5). So, arguably, the

> development of flight simulators provided an early example of the computer technology which allowed the boundaries between reality and simulation to become blurred: the images and information which furnish the material for exercises and war games become indistinguishable from what could be encountered in a real conflict.
>
> (Patton in Baudrillard 1995: 4)

But, while it is true that the war was conducted virtually, it is also true that there were many real casualties. And so, while on the one side politicians conducted a spectacle of war and soldiers fought their war as if they were playing a gigantic computer game, on the other side people were *really* dying.

In *Desert Rain*, the weak boundaries between reality and simulation were equally exposed, so that, in many ways, the viewer witnessed successions of slippages, contaminations even, of one world into the other. Even the very environment used for the performance was symptomatic of this choice. The space of *Desert Rain* felt immersive without being so. As indicated by Blast Theory, '[t]he rotating world is "leaking" over to the fabric walls by "mistake" not by intentional design. On the other hand the feeling and experience is that one is completely surrounded by water, light, graphics and sound' (Blast Theory 2002). And so, if on the one hand the viewer was under the illusion of being an onlooker, an audience, on the other the performance was continually pointing out to them that they themselves, like what they were watching, were also always inside the medium – that they could not just be an audience; that they too had participated in the making of this conflict.

As in other virtual-reality environments, the audience experienced some virtual events that left them feeling 'real' emotions. Clarke, for instance, summarises her feelings during the piece as follows: 'I am in no present danger, as I rationalize my participation, I am only navigating myself around symbols of danger. Yet in negotiating these symbols, I am energized, perplexed, uncertain, frightened. I inhabit a whole reality of emotion and experience' (Clarke 2001: 50).

Desert Rain suggested that the understanding of a virtual phenomenon as a non-phenomenon was incorrect. The main artistic concern of the piece was of course virtual warfare, whether as a game or as actual warfare. As suggested by Clarke, 'there are obvious allusions to the problematic association between computer game playing and military systems, the "dramatisation of life" that war seems to encapsulate and the pleasure taken from such effect' (Clarke in Blast Theory 2002). Here, the blurring of the boundaries between real and virtual events meant that the viewers ultimately did not know whether what they witnessed was derived from the news, a video game, a film, or was 'just' part of a piece of theatre. The most 'real' element of the piece was perhaps the discovery of the sand box, an event which for the majority of people took place long after the end of the performance, as if to say that whether what one saw was mediated or 'real', the long-lasting effect was the same. Baudrillard's reading of the figure of 100,000 Iraqi dead was that the

> dead still serve as an alibi for those who do not want to have been excited for nothing: at least the dead would prove that this war was indeed a war and not a shameful and pointless hoax, a programmed and melodramatic version of what was the drama of war.
>
> (Baudrillard 1995: 74)

Desert Rain addressed just that – the making and simulating of the drama of war, the potential of spectacularity, of 'hoax', and the possible inaction and even confusion that this may have caused. And, by exposing it, it allowed us to understand that, if something happens in the virtual, it does not mean that it does not also happen in the real and that in our society of spectacle it is virtuality that needs looking into, for it does affect the real – for it is *in* the real.

5

TOWARDS AN AESTHETIC OF VIRTUAL REALITY

Virtual reality is in a paradoxical relationship with the real. On the one hand, it is part of the real; yet, on the other, it has to be constructed as different from the real in order to be perceived as separate from it. Thus, virtual reality consists of a dichotomous paradox, torn between its ontological status which locates it as part of the real and its aesthetic, through which it demonstrates its difference from the real. From the point of view of perception, a viewer experiences this dichotomy as the principal characteristic of virtual reality. A viewer is both immersed within the virtual (in the sense that they are part of it) and interacting with it (and so they are separate from it). The consequence of this is that virtual reality is perceived as something both familiar and estranging, both known and unknown. Moreover, virtual reality can succeed only as it approaches presence. This means the viewer has to be put in a situation where they experience the virtual environment as becoming present. Thus, virtual reality has to be able to *double* the viewer's sense of location and experience, *and* accent it, to make a narrative of it. Subsequently, the experience of virtual reality is always fictional as well as 'real'.

In virtual reality, everything is text; HTML as well as VRML (Virtual Reality Modelling Language). As suggested by Lev Manovich, 'future users may experience [the Web] as one gigantic 3D world which will contain all other media, including text, inside itself' (Manovich 1995). Virtual reality offers fluid and open forms that allow for the viewer simultaneously to be inside and outside the work of art. The viewer is therefore always dispersed, and the work of art takes place through the dispersion and displacement thus caused. Moreover, upon entering virtual reality, the viewer becomes a cyborg, a fiction, as well as a creature of social reality (Haraway 1991: 149). So, not only do the viewers become part of the larger narrative of virtual reality; they also become actively involved in it. In other words, they do not so much perform in it as perform it. Virtual reality has to be embodied by the viewer in order to 'manifest' itself, so it is not independent from the viewer but caused and embodied by them. In other words, virtual reality is both inside and outside the viewer.

In representing a tool through which to read, view and experience the real, the virtual is able to offer the possibility of aesthetic, ethical and political discourse. So if the primary characteristic of virtual reality is its paradoxical relationship with the real, its second characteristic is the fact that this allows for ethical and political impact. Virtual reality is not only a medium, like television or film, but, like language, a medium that is able to reinvent itself and reflect upon itself continuously. In it, the viewer may not only experience their own performance of the medium, but may witness the medium's capacity to perform itself. And, if on the one hand virtual reality thus appears to be the most exciting, democratic or even global means of communication, on the other its capacity to simulate the real, to *stand for* the real, has major ethical and political consequences.

Today, virtual reality is one of Western society's primary tools to present and advertise itself, reflect on itself, create experience of itself that furthers knowledge and thus becomes art. This omnipresence of the World Wide Web in Western society implies that, in its philosophy and ethics, politics and art, it is today impossible to think about environment, nature and the 'real' without incorporating the virtual within whichever critical discourse is being utilised. In fact, the virtual has become the main theatre of the real – the place from where the real can be viewed, a space for critique, art and politics. And although its aesthetic is one of appearance, manifestation, 'arrival' (Virilio 1996: 131–2), its ontology is, like that of performance, one of 'disappearance' (Auslander 1999: 45). This leads to the second paradox of virtual reality: the dichotomy between its aesthetic and its ontology. Again, it is within this dichotomy that the ethical and political implications of 'being in the Web' lie.

But a virtual reality environment is much more than just a set of images or texts that manifests itself to us. First of all, the 'images' are the products of a montage that has taken place from within the world of the image (Popper 1993: 77). Thus, the image always also contains a trace of its maker (which in this case includes the artist or scientist as well as its operator and viewer). The virtual work of art thus exists in a multiplicity of locations and through a variety of agents. In computer-generated worlds, space is missing in the sense that 'the environment between objects', 'the effects of the objects on one another' and even 'an atmosphere which unites everything together' are missing (Manovich 1995). But virtual reality also produces distortions in time, given that applications are usually created out of time. The result is that the time/space distortion creates a tension with the 'real' through which the viewer is able to experience estrangement. Thus, virtual reality represents a spatio-temporal illusion whose task it is to appear different from the 'real' spatio-temporal illusion created by universally adopted spatio-temporal conventions. Yet the most exciting experience of virtual reality is not so much the one that totally alters the viewer's perspective on the real as the one that is able to expand, augment and enlarge the real. In other words, it is in its *relationship* with the real, rather than in its attempts to substitute itself for the real, that the most original use of virtual reality is found. So, ultimately, the main aesthetic feature of virtual reality is not so much the fact that it might represent an accident of the real (Virilio 1995) as the fact that it represents its theatre – the location from which the real can be viewed.

Dialectics in action – between real and simulated: Merce Cunningham and LifeForms

The well-known American dancer and choreographer Merce Cunningham started using LifeForms in 1989 and motion capture in 1997. LifeForms was developed at Simon Fraser University at the Computer Graphics and Multi-media Research Laboratory under the direction of Thomas Calvert. A computer tool designed specifically for dance choreography, it provides 'an interactive graphical interface that enables a choreographer or animator to sketch out movement ideas in space and time' (Schiphorst in Jacobson 1992: 147). It represents the body as a series of concentric circles through which movements of the arms, legs, torso and head can be programmed independently. Cunningham utilises the program as follows:

> [he] can dictate – and simultaneously notate – a wide variety of choreographic variables (everything from the flexing of a joint or the height and/or length of a jump, the location of each dancer on stage, the transition from one phrase to the next, etc.). The computer screen, divided into squares like a checkerboard, becomes a 'virtual stage' that can be electronically tilted or rotated so that the genderless, 'wire-frame'

LifeForm figures can be viewed from any number of perspectives.

(Copeland 1999: 42)

Cunningham claimed that 'working with LifeForms suggests possibilities of working with time and space that [he] had never thought of before' (Cunningham in Schiphorst 1997: 93). The program, which allows him to draw combinations of movements that might seem unnatural or even impossible for the human body to perform in the real, is not merely used as a notation system but as an alternative starting point, located outside the body, for the creation of movement in real time and space. As Cunningham suggests, in LifeForms, '[t]hings can happen that you think are impossible, but if you try them out, they lead you to something else. And it's all in space, not in time, you're looking visually and putting things in space' (*ibid.*). Thus, through LifeForms, as through other forms of virtual-reality technology, a dialectic is set up between the real and the virtual. This dialectic, however, does not tolerate a synthetic culmination, as the two antitheses are never quite allowed to come together. This leaves the viewer, who is already starting from a condition of dispersion, in a position from which they are never able to draw a synthesis of the two. In fact, put in this position, the viewer is forced to witness a consequence of the real and the virtual's inability to coincide and subsequently interpret the loss or excess that this faulty juxtaposition has produced.

Just a few years after starting to work with LifeForms, Cunningham wrote an essay entitled 'Four Events that Have Led to Large Discoveries' (1994) in which he listed the four moments that most influenced his work: 'the decision to separate music and dance'; the decision 'to use chance operations in the choreography'; 'the work we have done with video and film'; and 'the use of a dance computer, LifeForms' (Cunningham in Copeland 1999: 44). This shows that there is a progression from the dissociation of sound and image that Cunningham had been theorising and practising since the 1940s to the chance-generated compositional processes of a piece such as, for instance, *Untitled Solo* (1953), in which Cunningham's 'movement choices for the arms, legs, head, and torso were all conceived separately and ultimately linked together by chance operations [. . .] This collage-like conception of the body (as an inorganic "assemblage" of parts) anticipates the way a film or videotape editor arranges and re-arranges individual cuts and splices' (Copeland 1999: 44). Having used chance procedures in dance since the early 1950s, Cunningham then incorporated these procedures into the use of the computer through LifeForms. Cunningham's 'de-centered' organisation of the stage space 'has long provided a model for the sort of "liquid architecture" one now finds in the world of "hypertext" and the CD ROM – where multiple "windows" of information can be opened simultaneously in an overlapping collage of interactive choices' (*ibid*.: 45).

While LifeForms made it possible for Cunningham to continue working with chance and editing, it also allowed him to extend the use of space in his work to include virtuality as a process that was to be both part of and a counterpoint to the real. For Cunningham, as for his companion, the composer John Cage, the work of art could not be separated from the context in which it was created, performed and watched. So, for Cage, the very practice of art 'should introduce us to life' (Cage in Kaye 1994: 98) and this could happen only as 'a process, a resistance to the presence of the object' which involves an 'uncovering of the work's inherent instability' (Kaye 1994: 98). LifeForms allowed for the creation of movement that could be constructed using chance operations and did not have to take into account any of the variances of the real (especially, as Cunningham himself points out, time). This meant that Cunningham could work in an open, hypertextual way, but also that the 'resistance' in these works could be their ultimate unrealisability in time and space. In other words, the resistance could be the loss produced by the impossibility of the overlap of the real with the virtual.

Trackers (1991) was the first piece in which Cunningham used LifeForms. Chance procedures were used 'to determine how the body would move, what body parts would be used, and what shapes would be incorporated' (Schiphorst in Jacobson 1992: 153). The title refers to both camera and computer work (Copeland 1999: 50) and one-third of the movement was created with the computer so that it looked 'unnatural' (Johnson 1993–4: 28). So, for instance, 'Walker', a phrase taking place approximately sixteen minutes into the piece, was constructed using three separate iterations:

> [d]uring the first pass, Cunningham used a walking pattern which existed in the LifeForms menu, and began to alter the timing of the walking step pattern, by simply increasing or decreasing proportional timings between shapes in a direct visual way that leads Cunningham to say 'instead of thinking in time, you're looking visually and putting things in space'.

In this first iteration, the effect of increasing the spatial relationships between walking steps directly affected the timing
of the steps, causing a quirky, uneven, and distinctively odd
walking rhythm.

(Schiphorst 1997: 94)

During the second iteration, Cunningham added 'the arms without
referring to any relationship between what was occurring in the legs',
and in the third iteration, he 'added the torso and head to the phrase,
again without reference to what was occurring in the legs or arms'
(*ibid.*). Interestingly, dancers reported that the sequence was very difficult to learn because the movements were going 'against what the
body naturally did when it walked' (*ibid.*).

Similar dynamics took place in *Beach Birds* (1991), which, as in
other pieces elaborated via the computer, had the effect of destabilising and displacing 'our received ideas of the "human"' (Reynolds
2000). *Beach Birds*, which has been described as offering 'a vision of
heightened reality' (Kisselgoff in Reynolds 2000), looked like 'nature
run through a computer' (Weinstein in Reynolds 2000). Here,
through LifeForms, Cunningham presented 'the quirky fragmenta-
tions of the body, the oddly angled limbs and, at times, a quasi-robotic
rigidity and stiffness' (Reynolds 2000). The piece, in which the
different parts of the body – arms, legs and torso – were choreographed separately, captures a range of bird-like and human
movements, and adopts 'a whole vocabulary of familiar, angular
motions: twitching, jerking, hopping, leg shaking, wing stretching,
head cocking, group immobility, encroaching on one another's territory for territory or pairing' (Kendall in Reynolds 2000).

Cunningham's choreography displaces fixed categories (Reynolds
2000) and achieves the creation of an event in which nothing is
constructed and presented hierarchically. Thereby the choreographer
realises the *mise-en-scène* of a process of continuous transformation,
where everything is seen as *in fieri* (coming into being), and a series
of dialectical antitheses whose synthesis is never given or realised
is presented. Thus, for instance, the dancers in *Enter* (1992) are 'not
quite angels, but not quite human either. Something *in between*'
(Berman in Reynolds 2000, emphasis added). Interestingly, '[t]he title
Enter is no accident. It was inspired by what Cunningham called
"the most important button" on the keyboard' (August in Schiphorst
1997: 97). In this work, as in most virtual-reality artworks, one can
only enter, and then enter again and again the dichotomous worlds
that compose it – because, once the work is penetrated, no real

Figure 13 CRWDSPCR, 1996, Merce Cunningham Dance Company.
Photographer: Michael Stier. Courtesy of Cunningham Dance
Foundation.

progression or conclusion could ever wrap it to a close, since, once
entered, the story of the viewer's relationship with the artwork has
begun and the viewer can never quite leave it.

Likewise, *CRWDSPCR* (1993), pronounced 'crowd spacer'
(Caplan 1997: 100), suggests 'both utopia and chaos, humanity and
technology, in ways which undermine these oppositions' (Reynolds
2000). Here, the title of the piece 'playfully draws attention to
linguistic "spacing" through the removal of vowels, which are present
only virtually, through their absence, producing a "crowding" of the
letters themselves on the page' (*ibid.*). The title may in fact be read as
'crowd spacer' or 'crowds pacer', 'a twin reference to the way in
which technology has both crowded space and quickened pace'
(Copeland 1999: 51). As the title suggests, it 'is extremely difficult to
separate "individual" from "group" movements [since] the movement
impetus appears to be collective rather than individual, as if
"programmed" from outside, by natural or computerized processes'
(Reynolds 2000). The dancers' movement is clearly constructed in an
environment not defined by gravity, so it always looks alien, other.

In *CRWDSPCR*, the viewer witnesses the dancers executing
movements produced virtually that appear 'un-done', un-natural,

'unknown' (Cunningham 1996). The actualisation of these movements on stage, movements that have been created in space but not in time, creates a tension that is ultimately due to the resistance put forward by the body, which, of course, is in both space *and* time. In the real, duration and gravity determine progression and the virtually programmed 'real' body looks as if it is struggling with time, as if it is not quite *in* time. What is created in the virtual cannot comprehend all the parameters of the real, so it cannot entirely be perceived and located as 'real'. However, because the virtual is part of the real, it is in itself formed by what is already familiar, known. The virtual therefore always contains something that is already familiar – something that has already been experienced. This is why, upon entering a virtual-reality environment, the viewer usually *knows* what to do, even if they have never been in the environment before.

CRWDSPCR presents the dialectics of this tension between the real and the virtual in action (drama). Thus, the piece presents the conflict between the known, familiar movements of the dancers, and the unknown, unfamiliar (*unheimlich*) sequences developed through LifeForms. And herewith the piece shows how, in the complex relationship between the real and the virtual, the two never culminate into a synthesis and yet constantly strive to become each other. Here, as in most virtual-reality contexts, the relationship between the real and the virtual is one of desire (of wanting the other), cannibalism (of absorbing the other) and war (of annihilating the other). As dialectics in action, the relationship between virtual reality and the real is one of continuous transformation into the other. And thus virtual reality is in a constant state of flux. The virtual is in a condition of becoming; it is continually appearing because it has always already disappeared.

Full immersion: the CAVE

The term 'virtual reality' was coined by Jaron Lanier, and describes, as indicated in a more recent definition, 'a real or simulated environment in which the perceiver experiences telepresence' (Steuer 1992: 76–7). Often used as a synonym of cyberspace, which also refers to a simulated environment allowing for human interaction (Sterling 1990), it defines a process of simulation and the presence of a 'reality' that is produced artificially. The simulation is usually created by mounting a small pair of video monitors directly on the user's head. These form a stereoscopic image before the eyes which, as suggested by Michael Benedikt, is then continuously updated and readjusted by the computer to respond to head movements, so that the user finds themself totally surrounded by what appears to be a three-dimensional world (Benedikt 1993: 11). This sensation of being surrounded by, even immersed in, another world is perhaps what most strongly characterises the interaction between a given user and the phenomenon known as virtual reality.

The relationship between the real and the virtual is at the very heart of most studies of virtual reality. As pointed out by Michael Heim,

> [s]ensory immersion has broad ontological implications. First, virtual entities are not representations. They do not re-present. They do not 'present again' something that is already present somewhere else [. . .] As in the medieval theory of transubstantiation, the symbol becomes the reality. This is the meaning of telepresence.
>
> (Heim in Featherstone and Burrows 1995: 70)

When immersed in virtual reality, the user is not presented with a copy or imitation of the real, but rather with something that has its own ontological status. Because this virtual world is not a representation of the real, it must be part of it. And yet the virtual is not simply synonymous with the real. While it is part of the real, it does not coincide with it. It is neither unreal nor irreal, so it follows that it must be both *in* the real and yet *not* the real. This paradox, which explains virtual reality's unstable ontological status, allows for the creation of an art form that both utilises and subverts canonical conceptions of 'realness', 'realism' and even 'real'.

The virtual world is often reported as being able to draw the viewer into a false sense of perception. The virtual continuously borrows (copy – cut – paste) from the real in order to induce the viewer to believe that it is 'just like' the real. However, virtual-reality users often find that the virtual does not only borrow from the real, but cannibalises it, so that the virtual supersedes, or even substitutes itself for, the real. So, for instance, Heim describes experiencing an 'Alternate World Syndrome' after spending six hours in virtual reality at the Banff Centre for the Arts in Alberta, Canada. In virtual reality,

> [e]verything seems brighter, even slightly illusory. Reality afterwards seems hidden beneath a thin film of appearance. Perceptions seem to float over a darker, unknowable truth. The world vibrates with the finest of tensions, as if something big were imminent, as if you were about to break through the film of illusion.
>
> (Heim in Featherstone and Burrows 1995: 67)

As Allucquère Rosanne Stone explains, a similar feeling may develop simply by being in an online virtual environment, so that occasionally a person's online persona may become so 'finely' developed that it takes over their life off the Net (Stone in Benedikt 1993: 84).

This appropriation of the real by the virtual of course has wider political and ethical implications. The consequences of looking at the real through virtual-reality technologies became manifest during the first Gulf War, in which 'the screen became the scene of the war' (Robins and Levidow in Gray 1995: 120). During this conflict it became clear that the new video technology was able to create the feeling of a closer proximity between the weapon and the target while simultaneously producing a greater psychological distance, in that 'seeing was split off from feeling' and 'the visible was separated from the sense of pain and death', so much so that '[e]nemy threats – real or imaginary, human or machine – became precise grid locations, abstracted from their human context'. This 'was the ultimate voyeurism: to see the target hit from the vantage point of the weapon', 'to see from the bombers' perspective' (*ibid.*: 121 and 123).

Clearly, definitions of the real are no longer simply constituted by what is seen by the eyes, but also by what is seen through a microscope, a telescope and even the interface of one's computer screen. And, while on the one hand the virtual appropriates and cannibalises the real, the real is still our main point of reference in any definition and understanding of the virtual. Thus, Deborah Lupton, for instance, shows how popular and technical representations of computer viruses draw on discourses presenting computers as humanoid and embodied, so much so that viral computer infections are often described by employing the same vocabulary that is used for HIV and AIDS:

> there are a series of discourses that suggest that computers which malfunction due to 'viral contamination' have allowed themselves to become permeable, often via the indiscreet and 'promiscuous' behaviour of their users (in their act of inserting 'foreign' disks into their computer, therefore spreading the virus from PC to PC).
>
> (Lupton in Featherstone and Burrows 1995: 99)

So, interestingly, the greatest technological invention of our age is treated here not as a lifeless tool but rather as a new 'human', which, just like the old human, is prone to infection, contamination and even death. This suggests that while the human is tending towards a cyborgian, post-human existence, the computer is becoming increasingly human. In this sense, the real and the virtual are in a relationship of desire for each other as they attempt to possess and become one another.

Technically, virtual reality creates a simulated environment that may be experienced through the help of computer technology. As early as the 1960s, head-mounted displays were used to create the simulation of a reality that changed as the viewer moved through it. The main difficulty here was to 'create that basic relationship between your head and the outside world in order for virtual reality to simulate presence in a virtual space' (Lanier in Jacobson 1992: 272). This suggests that the virtual is always created in relation to the real and that the virtual *needs* the real as its major point of reference. The technological device that is most commonly used for the creation of an immersive virtual-reality environment is the head-mounted display that places a video screen in front of each of the viewer's eyes, thus filling the field of vision with a moving image so that '[e]ach eye is presented with a slightly different image, to create a three-dimensional illusion. When you move your head, the scene around you changes, just like in the physical world' (*ibid.*). Another commonly used tool is the dataGlove, which literally 'puts your hand inside the virtual space' (*ibid.*: 273), so that the viewer can touch and pick up virtual objects as if they were 'real'. Gloves may also offer a tactile feedback, so when the viewer touches the virtual object they *actually* feel something. Both the head-mounted display and the dataGlove act as body extensions, stretching the real body's capacity to perceive the 'real' world to include the virtual. Through them, the human subject is able to enter the world of augmented reality – and become a cyborg.

The North American artist Myron Krueger, one of the pioneers in the area of artificial reality, a term he himself coined in the mid-1970s (Krueger 1991: xiii), created one of the earliest examples of virtual reality in *Glowflow* (1961), developed by Dan Sandin, Jerry Erdman and Richard Venezky. The piece was a 'computer-controlled light–sound environment that had limited provision for responding to the people within it' (*ibid.*: 12). Viewers

> had amazing reactions to the environment. Communities would form among strangers. Games, clapping, and chanting would arise spontaneously. The room seemed to have moods, sometimes being deathly silent, sometimes raucous and boisterous. Individuals would invent roles for themselves [. . .] Since the GLOWFLOW publicity mentioned that the environment could respond to the viewers, many people

assumed that every visual pattern they saw and every sound
they heard was in response to what they personally were
doing the moment before, and they would leave convinced
that the room had responded to them in ways that it simply
had not.

(Krueger 1991: 15)

Although an early experiment, *Glowflow* displayed many of the characteristics of virtual environments. First, it offered the possibility
of an immersive experience. Second, it played with perception so
that, as Krueger indicates, the viewers were unsure about the degree
of responsiveness of the environment, thus creating some zones of
fluidity between the real and the virtual. Third, the piece was
theatrical in that it primarily represented a 'place for viewing'. Finally,
it offered a place for interaction, between the environment and the
viewers, between the virtual and the real, between the world as it
appears and the world as it is.

As suggested by Margaret Morse, '[t]he concept of "space" applied
to computer – and other machine-generated realms – is itself a
metaphor that invokes something quite different from the fundamental experience of being in a location in the physical world in a body
rooted to the ground by gravity' (Morse 1998: 178). In virtual reality,
the viewer is in one place and yet occupies different spaces. Moreover,
the technologies of virtual reality render any discourse on presence and
absence dichotomous, 'irrelevant' (Hayles in Druckrey 1996: 261). This
is because, in virtual reality, simulations are both present and not present, while viewers, too, are both inside and not inside the world of virtual reality (*ibid.*: 262). Thus, in virtual reality, body motions affect what
happens in the simulation so that 'one both is and is not present in the
body and in the simulation' (Hayles in Moser and MacLeod 1996: 14).
This suggests that in these complex simulated environments the viewer
is able to exist in fragmentation, in both the real and the virtual, as both
a subject (in the real) and an object (in the virtual), performing their
own presence (and therefore absence) in between the two worlds.

One of the most exciting and inventive virtual-reality environments
is the CAVE, developed by Tom DiFanti and Dan Sandin of the
Electronic Visualization Laboratory at the University of Illinois in
Chicago. The CAVE was premiered at the ACM SIGGRAPH 92
Conference, where it was presented as 'a virtual reality *theater*'
(Sandin in Janko, Leopoldseder and Stocker 1996: 85, emphasis
added). CAVE stands for CAVE Automatic Virtual Environment, a
title inspired by Plato's exploration of perception, illusion and reality

through the metaphor of the cave in *The Republic*. Sandin described the environment as a

> multi-person, room–sized, high–resolution, 3D video and audio environment. Graphics are rear projected in stereo onto three walls and the floor, and viewed with stereo glasses. As a viewer wearing a location sensor moves within its display boundaries, the correct perspective and stereo projections of the environment are updated, and the image moves with and surrounds the viewer.
>
> (Sandin in Janko, Leopoldseder and Stocker, 1996: 84)

In the CAVE, the viewer does not use the conventional head-mounted display but just a pair of lightweight polarised glasses. These allow them to see the polarised three-dimensional images that are projected on all the surfaces of the environment, and which are continually updated by the computer as the user moves through the virtual-reality programs. These graphics are projected to the left and then the right eye alternately at ninety-six images per second. A lead visitor can guide a group through a position-sensing device, while an interactive wand, a kind of 3D mouse, allows them to control the direction and movement. Here, the viewer can become part of a story and experience the virtual world from their own perspective. CAVEs are unique in that they allow multiple users to experience a given immersive virtual environment simultaneously:

> [t]he participant to the CAVE experiences an unprecedented sensation of immersion in a room–sized environment while navigating a wand which transports him or her from one part of a scene as well as from one of the many visually compelling, fanciful worlds which have been created for this system to another.
>
> (Goodman in Sommerer and Mignonneau 1998: 257–8)

CAVEs can be used commercially, by such companies as General Motors and Volkswagen, which employ the environment to study car design and build prototypes. Moreover, CAVEs are now used by medical researchers, who wish to explore the human body through virtual-reality applications, and NASA scientists, who have employed CAVEs in the space programme. However, since their inception, CAVEs have also been used in art programmes, such as Hisham Bizri and Maria Roussos's *Mythologies* (1998), which is based on the Cretan myth of the Minotaur, the Apocalypse of St John, Dante's *Inferno*, Albrecht Dürer's woodcuts after the Apocalypse and Jorge Luis Borges's *Library of Babel* (Stocker and Schöpf 1998: 218). Other well-known CAVE environments are Josephine Anstey and Dave Pape's *The Thing Growing* (1998), which has been described as a 'virtual Frankenstein experiment' (*ibid.*: 226) and Franz Fischnaller and Yesenia Maharaj Singh's *Multi Mega Book* (1997), which allows the viewer to turn the pages of a gigantic virtual book and move into the various worlds within, such as an idealised Renaissance city, where they may view a recreation of Leonardo's *Last Supper*, use Johannes Gutenberg's printing press and visit a digital city of the future.

Most CAVEs draw on photo-realism, but some are successfully adopting other styles. A well-known example of this is the cartoon-like *Crayoland* (1995), built by David Pape at the Electronic Visualization Laboratory at the University of Illinois, which allows the viewer to travel through a child-drawn landscape, complete with forest, flowers, buzzing bees and randomly flying butterflies. *Crayoland*,

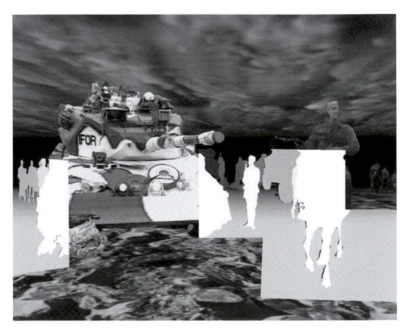

Figure 14 World Skin, 1997, Maurice Benayoun and Jean-Baptiste Barrière, Z-A.net/AEC/SGI.

comprising drawings of flat, two-dimensional objects that are encountered in a three-dimensional world, proved that the most effective environments were not necessarily those displaying the highest degree of 'realness', and that virtual presence was more dependent on behavioural or performative features than photo-realism.

The French artists Maurice Benayoun and Jean-Baptiste Barrière's *World Skin* (1998), for instance, does not draw on photo-realism and yet is one of the most disturbing virtual environments created for CAVE. Unlike other CAVE programs, *World Skin* has a strong and direct political tone that is strengthened by the fact that, in the CAVE, it is the viewer who performs the work of art. After entering *World Skin* through the immersive landscape of the CAVE, visitors find themselves in 'a war-ravaged area in which they can move through wasteland scenes of destruction' (Wilson 2002: 705). Benayoun describes this moment as follows:

> [a]rmed with cameras, we are making our way through a three-dimensional space. The landscape before our eyes is scarred by war-demolished buildings, armed men, tanks and artillery, piles of rubble, the wounded and the maimed. This arrangement of photographs and news pictures from different zones and theatres of war depicts a universe filled with mute violence. The audio reproduces the sound of a world in which to breathe is to suffer.
>
> (Benayoun in Wilson 2002: 706)

Despite the scene of devastation, and the immersive quality of the piece, there is something estranging in this environment that stops the viewer from becoming emotionally involved. This CAVE environment is

> not realistic in the usual sense. Something is wrong about this world: there is a horrible abstraction. Even though depth is everywhere, many of the persons and items in the landscape are rendered almost flat, like stage props. These flats sit in 3-D space in relation to each other. The colour is polytonal only within restricted parts of the spectrum, for example, shades of brown.
>
> (Wilson 2002: 705)

Upon entering the piece, visitors are given their glasses, but also, unusually for a CAVE environment, a camera, with which they are encouraged to take pictures of the war zone. Benayoun comments:

[l]ike so many tourists, we are visiting it with camera in hand. Each of us can take pictures, capture a moment of this world that is wrestling with death. The image thus recorded exists no longer. Each photographed fragment disappears from the screen and is replaced by a black silhouette. With each click of the shutter, a part of the world is extinguished. Each exposure is then printed out.

(Benayoun in Wilson 2002: 707)

Although the viewer is immersed within one of the most sophisticated virtual environments ever constructed, they encounter only two-dimensional silhouettes, nothing but *images* of war, representations that they themselves can literally obtain and keep for their own consumption. In Benayoun's words, '[w]e take pictures [. . .] we rip the skin off the body of the world. This skin becomes a trophy' (Benayoun in Wilson 2002: 707): a sample of the skin of the world.

As the visitor progresses through this environment, they find that there is no dramatic storyline, no progression or real change. The same images return repeatedly, following an endless fractal cycle. As Benayoun points out, '[t]he farther we penetrate into this universe, the more strongly aware we become of its infinite nature. And the chaotic elements renew themselves, so that as soon as we recognize them, they recompose themselves once again in a tragedy without end' (in Wilson 2002: 707). While the sound of the clicking cameras becomes increasingly threatening, the viewer finds that as they photograph the images (*take* the images), these disappear from the program: 'here photography is a weapon of erasure' (*ibid.*). As the viewers watch the performance of war from within the performance, they, too, find themselves at war, transformed into virtual-reality killers. And as the world of CAVE creates 'the illusion of presence' (Wilson 2002: 620) only to take it apart again, we, too, are made to reflect about ourselves, shooting away with our cameras, eating up the world of the image without quite knowing what is going to appear from behind it. According to Benayoun, '[h]ere, being engulfed by war is an immersion into a picture, but it is a theatrical performance as well. In the sequence of events which characterise the story of a single person, war is an exceptional incident which reveals humanity's deepest abyss' (Benayoun and Barrière in Stocker and Schöpf 1997: 313). In this theatre of war, Benayoun and Barrière create a performance around the viewer's growing awareness that not only do media have the power to create as well as destroy the world of the image, but that this virtual activity has a very direct impact on the real. By creating a link between the virtual and the real, in that the pictures taken may be collected outside the CAVE after the viewing, Benayoun and Barrière expose the fact that events taking place during an immersion in the virtual may have consequences that affect the viewer in the real.

In virtual reality, the viewer's focus is on the virtual, in which they are temporarily immersed. Aesthetically, the virtual consists of a near-perfect illusion of the real. Interestingly, it is in this unwillingness to overlap with the real that the strength of the virtual lies. The more perfect the illusion, the stronger the impact on the real, because the virtual, in order to appear as virtual, has to be affecting the viewer in the real. And, of course, to affect the viewer in the real, the virtual must produce a 'fake' distance from the real so that the real can be perceived as separate from it. Subsequently, the main characteristic of a virtual-reality immersion is not so much its skill in simulating the real, but rather its ability to estrange the viewer from the real, thereby interfering with their capacity to see and consequently read the real. This is why, after a virtual-reality experience, coming back to the real seems both strange and estranging. And this is also why the virtual is able to act as a theatre of the real, a place of *Verfremdung*, and therefore ultimately of reflection.

The politics of interactivity: Lynn Hershman and Guillermo Gómez-Peña

Since the real and the virtual can never quite coincide, it is in creating the perspective and the viewpoint from which to observe the real (from the virtual) and vice versa that the scientist and artist dealing with virtual reality is inevitably adopting a political stance. Everything that has to do with virtual reality has political consequences and is therefore a more or less direct act of politics. By dealing with the creation of viewpoint, the artist or scientist who engages with virtual reality is in effect deciding how the user is to view the spectacle of the real. In other words, the artist or scientist creating virtual reality decides not only what the viewer sees and experiences in the virtual but how exactly this is to affect the viewer in the real.

A number of practitioners have endeavoured to expose the politics embedded in the use of virtual reality. Among them, the North American artist Lynn Hershman and the Mexican artist Guillermo Gómez-Peña have created some of the most exciting, inspiring and politically stimulating work to date. Their commitment to the exposure of the ethical and political consequences of using virtual reality has manifested itself throughout their works, and is especially evident

in their exposure of interactivity as a non-neutral tool and, in Gómez-
Peña's case, in the denunciation of the World Wide Web as a
politically charged medium. Through their works, it is possible to
conclude that neither the artwork nor the viewer is starting from a
position of neutrality, and that the relationship between the two, seen
through the medium of virtual reality, is in itself politically charged.

Lynn Hershman's *Lorna* (1982) was one of the earliest interactive
environments that engaged with non-linear film narrative. The viewer
was seated in an area imitating a small and slightly claustrophobic
lounge, containing furniture, a television set and personal objects, such
as a fish bowl and pictures. Here, they could interact with the television set by selecting specific objects on the screen and clicking on
them with a remote control. By exploring the scenarios behind these
objects, the viewer was able to put together the story of Lorna, a
woman living in loneliness and desperation. The only contact Lorna
had with the world was through her television, just as the only contact
the viewer had with Lorna was through the television set of the installation. The story was constructed through various plot-lines, and the
viewer's decisions determined the plot's actual development (Dinkla
1997: 191). In Hershman's words, 'the action was literally in [the
viewer's] own hands' (Hershman 2003).

The installation worked like a hypertext, and in the video the furniture had details that it did not have in the real. This slippage between
the virtual and the real, which were presented as similar but not iden-
tical, manifested itself in the fact that in the virtual the bowl contained
a fish that was not present in the real, and, likewise, the virtual drawers
were full of papers whereas in the real the drawers were empty (Dinkla
1997: 191). Through *Lorna*, Hershman thus drew the viewer's attention to the fact that everything in Lorna's life had been swallowed by
the world of the medium, and that during the process of mediation
'real' detail had been lost, so that ultimately the real and the virtual
could not be seen as overlapping. Here, the virtual, mediatised world
constitutes Lorna's 'real'. In other words, the virtual (Lorna's real) has
more detail than the real (the viewer's real).

In *Lorna*, the spectator becomes a voyeur, reconstructing Lorna's
life from the real and virtual objects in the real and virtual rooms
(Dinkla 1997: 191). Moreover, from the loss of real detail through
the process of mediation, the viewer is able to draw further information about Lorna as a being existing through mediation alone. And
while the viewer could carefully move through the plot of Lorna's
fragile existence, they themself could also become the focus of other
viewers' attention. It is possible for further viewers not only to watch

Lorna's life on the television screen, but to observe the 'active' viewer's interaction with her. Watching Lorna thus includes the possibility of seeing not only Lorna's life, but the viewer's reconstruction of her life. Interestingly, navigating the piece is quite difficult because of the multiple variations offered by the plot and because the plot includes the possibility of being caught 'in repeating dream sequences' (Anon 1994: 3). Here, '[t]he medium is the person' (Schwarz 1997: 123) and everything the viewer does or sees is received through the medium; that is, it is *inside* the medium. This is reflected in the fact that the storyline offers three possible outcomes: 'Lorna shoots her television set, commits suicide, or, what we Northern Californians consider worst of all, she moves to Los Angeles' (Hershman 2003). Here, even death comes through the medium (Schwarz 1997: 123): Lorna may only destroy the television set, thus ending her relationship with the outside world; commit suicide, which again implies the end of the medium; or move to Los Angeles, the city of Hollywood, the hyperreal – mediatisation.

Hershman's *Roberta Breitmore* (1972–82) has been described as 'an early excursion into virtuality, straddling the boundary between fiction and reality, or art and life' (Rötzer in Schwarz and Shaw 1996: 136). Roberta was 'at once artificial and real. She had a history which continually wrote itself anew, registering and documenting real experience, and leaving tangible traces of its existence' (*ibid.*). In *Roberta Breitmore*, Hershman herself became Roberta, thus creating a persona who had an identity, a physical embodiment, and even 'a set of individual gestures, needs and fears' (*ibid.*). Roberta had credit cards and an apartment, she corresponded with people and established relationships with them. She even put a small announcement in a newspaper in which she advertised for a roommate. The people who replied to the advert then became part of her fiction (Hershman Leeson 1996: 330). Hershman indicates that Roberta accumulated forty-three letters from individuals and had twenty-seven adventures. She also points out that

> [h]er childhood data was established before she was released into the world. ROBERTA reflected the values of her culture. She penetrated trends such as EST, WEIGHT-WATCHERS and most significantly, experienced resonant nuances of alienation. Roberta saw a psychiatrist, had her own language and handwriting, apartment and clothing, gestures and moods.
>
> (Hershman 2003)

Described as the 'private performance of a simulated persona', Roberta was 'at once artificial and real' (Hershman Leeson 1996: 330). In the Internet project related to the figure of Roberta, her fictional persona is 'designed as an updated Roberta' who not only navigates the Internet but is herself a creature of the Internet, a cyberbeing. Here, '[s]urveillance, capture and tracking are the DNA of her inherently digital anatomy. They form the underpinning of her portrait' (*ibid.*: 336). Thus, whereas in *Roberta Breitmore* Hershman was clearly *performing* Roberta, in the Internet version of the piece Hershman's 'performance' was curiously invisible, since on the Internet everybody, not just Roberta, embraces character and adopts one or multiple personae.

Hershman's subsequent piece *America's Finest* (1993–5) is an interactive installation in which the viewer encounters a rifle located upon a pedestal. Upon trying to use the rifle, the viewer sees a montage of pictures that includes a child, historical photographs from conflicts in which the rifle has been used, images from the museum or gallery walls in which the piece is located and finally themselves, seen from a variety of angles, while they are pointing the rifle. The weapon is the M-16, which was used in Korea, Vietnam and the first Gulf War. It is interactive, and simply by looking through the 'scope and pulling the trigger, the viewer 'enters the field of fire' (Hershman 2003). Here, the role of the killer and the victim are not only intertwined (Dinkla 1997: 194) but reversed (Hershman 2003). Thus, Hershman points out that in *America's Finest*, '[i]f you shoot [. . .] the child's face appears with a target drawn on it in red' (*ibid.*), while a voice says, 'Don't', 'It's easy', 'Shoot!' or 'Don't shoot please' – hence temporarily transforming the viewer into an active perpetrator. But the position of the viewer is rendered more complex by the fact that they themself also appear on the screen, as if they had been suddenly spotted by another sniper and were just about to be shot. So, 'pulling the trigger turns the viewer into both an aggressor and a subsequent victim of his/her own actions' (*ibid.*). Nobody is innocent in this work, since the viewer is located simultaneously inside and outside the installation, inside the virtual *and* in the real, so that a split, *double* existence is achieved, and the final realisation that virtual conflict has consequences in the real is made possible.

From *Lorna*, in which the viewer was responsible for the creation (and termination) of the plot of Lorna's life, to *Roberta Breitmore*, in which the viewer could interact and thus be part of the creation of the life of the 'real' persona of Roberta, to *America's Finest*, in which the viewer thinks they are simply positioning a weapon in a gallery

Figure 15 America's Finest, Lynn Hershman.

only to find out that by that very act they themself become per-petrators and victims of violence and war, Hershman's work prob-lematises the viewer's position by exposing the way in which interactivity creates choices that in themselves have political conse-quences and reveals how this affects identity in the virtual and the real world. Identity, Hershman notes, is 'the first thing you create when you log on to a computer service. By defining yourself in some way, whether through a name, a personal profile, an icon, or a mask, you also define your audience, space, and territory' (Hershman Leeson 1996: 325). Thus, online, everyone is performing, which is why

> [m]asks and self-disclosures are part of the grammar of cyber-space. They are the syntax of the culture of computer-mediated identity, which can include simultaneous multiple identities or identities that abridge and dislocate gender and age. One of the more diabolical elements of entering CMC or virtual reality is that people can only recognise each other when they are electronically disguised. Truth is precisely based on the inauthentic!
>
> (Hershman Leeson 1996: 325)

Here, Hershman draws attention to one of the paradoxes of cyber-space: the more sophisticated the fake (simulation), the more authentic (and 'truthful') it appears. Thus, cyberspace is not so much a place for authenticity and truthfulness, but rather the site of simulation, artifice and performance. In other words, it is the very theatre of the real.

A similar position is adopted by Guillermo Gómez-Peña, who argues that the Internet 'cannot be separated from the larger socio–political context in which it sits' (Gómez-Peña in Wilson 2002: 589). Throughout his work with new technologies, Gómez-Peña has exposed the political and ethical nature of cyborg interaction and chal-lenged the assumption that the World Wide Web is a vehicle for open and democratic communication. Thus, in *El Naftaztec: Cyber TV for 2000 AD* (1994) Gómez-Peña created 'a spoof in which it seemed Indian "pirates" had seized the airwaves to talk about Mayan innova-tions in cyber culture. The event was also broadcast on the Internet Mbone, and viewers were encouraged to send messages back' (*ibid.*). Here, and in later work, Gómez-Peña exposed the racism and pre-judice embedded in Western culture by openly allowing viewers to voice their concerns on the Web. Similar strategies were adopted in *Ethno-Cyberpunk Trading Post* (1995), in which the performer James Luna and Gómez-Peña transformed themselves each day 'into different performance personae such as The Shame-Man, The Postmodern Zorro, El Aztec High-Tech, El Cultural Transvestite, El Natural Born Asesino, etc.' while the performer Roberto Sifuentes, with whom Gómez-Peña has collaborated on a number of performances, was costumed as 'CyberVato, a robo-gang member consumed by fake and real techno-gadgetry'. The details of these transformations were broadcast live on the Web so that Internet users who saw both the webpage and the webcast of the live performance could 'send in images, sounds, and texts about how [they felt] Mexicans, Chicanos and Native Americans should look, behave, and perform in the 1990s'. The viewers' responses were then shown on gallery monitors manipulated by techno-disc-jockey CyberVato, and 'informed the ever-changing personae created by James and myself' (Gómez-Peña 1999: 57).

Interestingly, Gómez-Peña remarked that he received a profound response to this and other techno-diorama projects, and that by August 1998 his site had received over 20,000 hits, with thousands of replies being of a 'uniquely confessional nature' (Gómez-Peña 1999: 58). The popularity of this project and the nature of the response prompted the artist to note:

> [t]he total anonymity offered by the internet, along with the invitation to discuss painful and sensitive matters of race and identity in an artificially safe environment, seems to allow forbidden or forgotten zones of the psyche to surface. In a sense, through digital technology, we are enabling thousands of internet users to involuntarily collaborate with us in the creation of a new socio-cultural mythology of the Latino and the Indigenous 'Other'.
>
> (*ibid.*)

With this, Gómez-Peña draws attention to one of the fundamental characteristics of the Web: although it feels like a secure and enclosed environment, probably because of its friendly interface, it is in fact a very public arena. Because of the privacy and safety of the environment from which the viewer tends to operate, and the possibility of anonymity (although in real terms complete anonymity is of course impossible), the Internet viewer tends to abandon social and ethical etiquette, political correctness and even ethics, and adopt a position of excess, extremity. In other words, on the Web, the viewer starts from a position of safety (utilising the Web as a safety 'net') and ends up in a public arena, a postmodern and hyper-real *polis* in which everything is public and hence political. But, whereas in 'real' life users

Figure 16 Mexterminator, Guillermo Gómez-Peña.

would not openly admit to their prejudice and racism, on the Web they confess to it, seemingly without too much shyness or remorse. In *Mexterminator* (1998), viewers first encounter

the ominous figure of Cybervato (Roberto Sifuentes) gazing implacably through the viewfinder of a cybernetic headpiece. Wearing a red bandanna and blood-stained shirt rent through with bullet holes, he sits on a throne-like chair encrusted with computer circuit boards, which he periodically consumes. A large screen behind the platform on which he is displayed projects computer-mediated images, which he controls by manipulating a keyboard on his dais. With one arm encased in a metal prosthesis that terminates in weapon-sharp spikes and built-in coke spoon, and a similar prosthetic device attached to one leg, Cybervato (aka *homo chicanus*, ethnocyborg #209) appears as a techno-*rasquache* gangmember imperfectly assimilated by Borg drones.

(Wolford 1999: 59)

At the other end of the exhibition hall,

Mexterminator (Guillermo Gómez-Peña) sits resplendent on a custom-designed 'lowrider wheelchair', with red upholstery and glistening chrome. Wearing a gas mask crowned with pseudo-native feather headdress and holding a macabre, skull-faced scepter, he appears as a kind of post-apocalyptic shaman and political leader, presiding over a landscape decimated by war [. . .] Identified as *homo fronterizus*, ethnocyborg #187, he is characterized as an illegal border crosser and cultural invader, indestructible defender of immigrants' rights.

(*ibid.*)

Mexterminator was informed by the response of Internet users to a questionnaire posted on the performance's website. The responses were incorporated into the performance through the use of gallery monitors manipulated by CyberVato. Moreover, the performance allowed for 'an online forum in which issues of race and culture were debated in a *frank* manner' (Wolford 1999: 59, emphasis added). Samples of questions asked are: 'Where do aboriginal peoples belong? On the reserve or in the city? Where do Mexicans belong? In Mexico or everywhere? Do you think that Mexicans in the US are enjoying undeserved privileges?' (*ibid.*). Viewers were also asked to name 'real or imagined sexual encounters with Latinos, Native Americans and other persons of colour', 'to relate their wildest experience in a Third World country' and share 'their favourite racist joke' (*ibid.*: 61).

The 'Techno-Ethno-Graphic Profile', a wider questionnaire used by the performers, is published on the Web, and again includes such questions as do you think that political correctness has gone too far? do you often ask yourself, 'what happened to beautiful art that *everyone* can appreciate?' Please send us an image and/or description of an action you wish to have an authentic Mexican and/or Indian performance artist execute for you. Send your photos, drawings, images, music, sounds, etc. and 'The Shame-Man', 'El Mexican't' and 'CyberVato' will act out your fantasies. In the coming days, they will become a 'composit reflection' of your interracial desires.

(Gómez-Peña 1996; original emphasis)

Through this questionnaire, which acted as a 'barometer of the intolerance of other cultures' (Sifuentes in Gómez-Peña 1998), the performers collated the viewers' racist and prejudiced opinions and acted them out in a courageous act of political confrontation. This possibility of interaction was further extended to the live performance by the fact that the performers allowed the viewers to interact with them, and, in Gómez-Peña's words, 'feed us, touch us, smell us, massage us, braid our hair, take us for walks on dog leashes, or point prop weapons at us to experience the feeling of shooting at a real, live Mexican' (Gómez-Peña 2000: 55). Thus,

the personae displayed in these exhibits both cite and comment on stereotypes of Latinos and Native peoples, effectively invoking the ambivalence at the heart of colonial discourse by simultaneously embodying what spectators 'always already know' about Mexicans and Chicanos and highlighting the reductive and fixed nature of these projections by magnifying alleged attributes of Latino cultural others – such as hypersexuality, violence, drunkenness and archaic wisdom – to the point of absurdity.

(Wolford 1999: 60)

What Gómez-Peña achieves so brilliantly in his work is the exposure of how virtual reality unleashes a confessional mode so that individuals' intolerance and prejudice are made visible and then embodied via the performative process. His work

is very much about seduction and the destruction of that illusion [. . .] I want the audience to see and understand the mechanisms of cross-cultural fascination. I want to subvert that fascination by putting a mirror in the face of the audience so that what it sees is not the other but itself.

(Gómez-Peña in Wolford 1999: 60)

Through the creation of the ethno-cyborgs, the 'performance personae that incorporate narratives and images submitted by the anonymous Internet users' (Wolford 1999: 61), Gómez-Peña returns to the viewer their own image, rendered 'more' visible by the performative process. Like other cyborgs, this ethno-cyborg is 'a creature of social reality as well as a creature of fiction' (Haraway 1991: 149), constituted by both multiplicity and difference. Through this process of assimilation, Gómez-Peña literally embodies the racism and becomes the 'other', the viewer, presenting himself through a double layer that sees him, a 'real' Mexican, acting as the ethno-cyborg produced by the Internet users' representations of 'a real Mexican'.

In this extraordinary juxtaposition and exposure of the real through the virtual and the culturally constructed fiction of race and gender, cyborg and human, Gómez-Peña turns his 'real' persona inside out, so that the viewer may see the paradoxes, intolerances and racism so deeply embedded in Western culture. Because virtual reality is always constructed by the human, it is also always the repository of humankind's dreams, ambitions, longings, culture, ethics, intolerances, prejudices, racism, violence and, of course, ultimately its politics. This is why the virtual is never only a space for aesthetic and scientific innovation, but also the site of politics and ethics.

CONCLUSION

There is not one virtual theatre, but many. This is not only because of the variety of virtual art forms that can claim a certain degree of theatricality, but because the medium of virtuality itself acts as a theatre, a viewing point of the real. Increasingly, scientists endeavouring to explore the mysteries of human life, creating transportation that could take human beings to other worlds, or even simply creating better products for everyday consumption, are adopting virtual reality as a means of testing the conditions of the real. Thus, virtual reality is increasingly utilised as a laboratory to recreate the real. In this sense, virtuality is not only representing the main 'other' to the real, an other that is able to simulate the real while maintaining its difference from it, but can stand in for the real, thereby ultimately representing a perfect rehearsal space for it. Hence, virtual reality is both in the real and a simulation of the real. In other words, it is both the practice of the real and its theatre. And it is its paradoxical nature, caused by the contradiction between its ontology and its aesthetic, that makes it such an important site for both life and art.

Virtual reality is not only a rehearsal space and a theatre, but an archive, a place of memory, a repository for humankind's past, present and future plans, activities, dreams and failures. This is evident in Mark Napier's *The Shredder* (1998), which exposes HTML by altering codes before they are read by browsers. Here, '[c]ontent becomes abstraction. Text becomes graphics. Information becomes art' (Weibel and Druckrey 2001: 77). *The Shredder* dismantles the illusion of the World Wide Web as a 'physical page' (*ibid.*). As Napier himself suggests, the aim of the work is to find 'a way around the rules of the software to get behind the superficial appearance of the Web and to break down the appearance of solidity' (Napier in Baumgärtel 2001: 186). Appropriating and exposing the Web as a mass of HTML code, *The Shredder* thus 'dematerialises the web' and acts as 'a voracious public artwork' (Leopoldseder and Schöpf 1999: 46). *The Shredder* itself has no content: it is without 'message'; it even opens, literally, with a blank screen (*ibid.*). Only by entering the site and participating in the interface does the viewer both 'create' and 'complete' the work of art (*ibid.*). Moreover, within the world of *The Shredder*, the work poses 'as a browser, [. . .] prompts the user for a URL, then appropriates that web page to use as a raw material for its own fragmented output. It exposes the frailty of a medium that relies on software instructions to create the appearance of a consistent environment' (*ibid.*). In other words, *The Shredder* simulates the World Wide Web's capacity to store and present data to expose not only the fragility of the interface but the fragility of the simulation itself. Here, the program's code subverts the World Wide Web's 'usual' capacity to simulate the real, and thereby transforms mere data into art. As in Jodi's work, it is the modification or even the destruction of the code's ability to 'mean', to 'simulate', that transforms it into art.

Similar dynamics take place in Napier's *Digital Landfill* (1997), which has been described as a 'virtual compost heap' and a 'work of automated pop art' (Baumgärtel 2001: 182). Here, the viewer may copy data from their computer or another website and 'dump' them into the landfill site. The data then reappear as a series of various layers on the computer monitor, thus creating a collective 'art work' (*ibid.*: 183). Napier, who claims to be influenced by Jackson Pollock and Cy Twombly (*ibid.*: 184), explains that much of his work 'deals with the nature of ownership and authority in the online world' (*ibid.*: 186) and that both projects intend to hack websites: 'I make these art works to explore the mutability of the Web and to show how the browser imposes many of our real-world assumptions into the virtual world, where those assumptions really no longer apply' (Napier in Baumgärtel 2001: 186). In both *The Shredder* and *Digital Landfill*, Napier thus exposes the World Wide Web's ability to store and modify data 'neutrally', and suggests that in dealing with the Web we all still apply 'real-world assumptions' to it. But, although the Web is inextricably linked to the real world, it is also invariably different from it. It is precisely the aesthetic, ontological and ethico-political status of this difference that constitutes the most important aspect of the study of virtual reality.

Another crucial characteristic of the virtual is its ability to absorb and distort the real. Alba d'Urbano focused on this in her piece *Touch Me* (1995), comprising an interactive sculpture through which the viewer sees part of a female face on a monitor slowly transform into

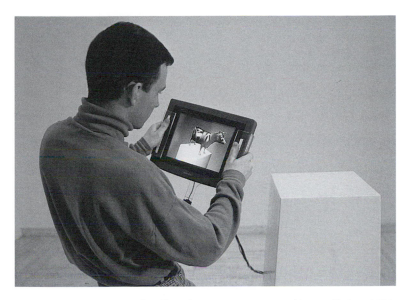

Figure 17 *The Golden Calf,* Jeffrey Shaw, computer-graphic installation, 1994, © Jeffrey Shaw, Institute for Visual Media, ZKM/Centre for Art and Media Karlsruhe.

themself (Schwartz 1997: 158). Likewise, in Jeffrey Shaw's *The Golden Calf* (1994), the real and the virtual are so intertwined that it becomes impossible for the viewer to tell them apart. *The Golden Calf* comprises a white pedestal upon which a portable computer screen is based. The viewer is encouraged to pick up the screen, and upon doing so sees on it a computer-generated image of a golden calf standing on the pedestal. By moving around the real pedestal, the viewer sees the virtual calf on the virtual pedestal from various angles. Shaw points out that 'the monitor functions like a window that reveals a virtual body apparently located physically in the real space' (Shaw 2002). However, not only does the real pedestal not have a calf standing on it, but the virtual pedestal is not a precise replica of the real one. In an 'interplay of imagination, presence and absence' (Weibel in Duguet, Klotz and Weibel 1997: 17), *The Golden Calf* thus implodes the real and the virtual into one artwork without allowing for either synthesis or catharsis. Although the virtual is able to absorb and distort the real, it never strives for a synthetic relationship with it. Thus, *The Golden Calf* has been described as '[t]wo faces that cannot be collapsed into one but remain in constant touch' (Duguet in Duguet, Klotz and Weibel 1997: 46). Shaw himself notes that *The Golden Calf* has a shiny mirror-like surface in which the viewer sees reflections of the actual venue of the installation [. . .] While the viewer is not included in this digitalised reflection of the environment, he does see himself reflected on the glass surface of the LCD screen [. . .] When moving the monitor screen up, down and round the pedestal, the viewer performs what looks like a ceremonial dance around a technological pilaster constructing an almost tangible phantasm.

(Shaw 2002)

The Golden Calf exposes a number of the characteristics of the relationship between the real and the virtual: first, one simulates the other but they do not coincide with each other; second, the virtual has to be performed ('danced', in this case), to become visible or active; third, the performance of the virtual is in itself an act of theatre because it allows the viewer (and possibly any other spectator who may find themself in the proximity of the viewer) to look at the real from a distance.

In viewing the real through the virtual, the viewer inevitably encounters the real and thus also themself. This feature of virtual reality is interestingly explored in Monika Fleischmann and Wolfgang Strauss's *Rigid Waves* (1993) and *Liquid Views* (1993), two interactive installations dealing with Ovid's myth of Narcissus. The former consists of a computer-controlled video wall which becomes an interactive surface and offers 'an encounter of the observer with himself. He himself is the interface with which he interacts' (Fleischmann and Strauss in Schwarz and Shaw 1996: 218). The artists describe the piece as follows: 'when the observer approaches, he sees only a reflection, which does not correspond to his normal perception. He sees himself as an impression, a body with tangled movements and finally as an image in a mirror, which breaks as soon as he comes too near' (*ibid.*: 218–19). Thus, *Rigid Waves* 'is an image in the image where the visitor meets himself. He himself is the interface he is acting with' (Fleischmann 1995). The encounter of the viewer with themself is rendered more complex by the fact that it is explicitly mediatised and thus fictionalised. Hence, the image the viewer sees first is described as 'impressionistic', becomes 'realistic' and finally, upon drawing even closer to the artwork, is 'smashed', leaving only an impressionistic 'shadow', or trace (*ibid.*). In other words, although in this virtual environment the viewer meets nothing but their own self, they are not discovering anything new, but simply witnessing the manifestation of the trace of their own presence. They are witnessing the fact that they were indeed there.

CONCLUSION

Likewise, in *Liquid Views*, or *The Virtual Fountain of Narcissus*,

> [t]he visitor approaches and sees his image reflected in the water – embedded in a fluid sphere of digital imagery. He tries to intervene, to touch the water surface, and generates new ripples. Increasing the water movement too much, over-stepping his limits, the viewer distorts his telematic reflection [. . .] After a time, while not touched, the water movement becomes calm again and returns to a liquid mirror.
>
> (Fleischmann 1995)

Here, 'the subject is the fountain in which Narcissus finally recognises himself. First of all [the viewer] thinks the water is a *you* – another being present' (Fleischmann and Strauss in Schwarz and Shaw 1996: 219, original emphasis). In other words, upon approaching the water, the viewer thinks of a mirror surface and its capacity to reflect the present. Only after some time do they discover that the reflection they see is virtual, that the water is an interface, and that what they see is in the past:

> [e]nticed by the water simulation, by their own image or by the sound of water, most visitors touch the 'surface of the water' immediately, which is in reality a touch-sensitive glass surface, which causes the image to disintegrate when touched. The observer of the installation does not notice that we can observe him. He feels unobserved and behaves freely. The computer, however, is able to store the images secretly, thus returning the visitor's facial expressions and behaviour. The fact of seeing without noticing that one is being seen is also a metaphor for using the internet.
>
> (Fleischmann and Strauss in Schwarz and Shaw 1996: 219)

Liquid Views is a metaphor not only for the use of the World Wide Web and its capacity to manipulate and control the real, but also for the fact that in a virtual-reality experience the path of a given user's itinerary is pre-written, pre-designed. In other words, virtual reality is not an objective reality but someone's work of art, in which a space for the viewer has been left more or less open.

Clearly, the future of humanity lies in its ability to utilise media, virtual reality in particular, as parts of everyday life. Our future may be dependent on how we utilise virtual reality to improve everyday-life conditions, or even to hide them. Thus, Jaron Lanier suggests that, in the future, our physical dwellings 'would probably be cheap, dull, unadorned shelters generated by robot factories to put no-frills roofs over the heads of an overpopulated humanity' and that 'to compensate for the squalid physical surroundings, VR will provide interactive virtual buildings for personal expression and aesthetic fantasy' (Lanier in Heim 1994: 1). If we agree with Lanier, virtual reality may become just as relevant as the 'real' in determining levels of comfort, aesthetic pleasure and even general well-being. Moreover, the plotting of the human genome has transformed the human being into mere information, a code just like HTML or VRML that can become the object as well as the subject of art. And, just as the body is extended and integrated into the machine, the machine may now integrate biological matter into its mechanisms (Palumbo 2000: 31). Through the use of virtual reality and the creation of the hypersurface, virtuality and reality have found a location for cohabitation in which, while maintaining their separate identities and avoiding synthesis, they can be experienced in their interrelatedness. Just as in future cinema we will be able to navigate our way through different environments, select those of our choice, interact with the characters and even enter the plot (Murray 1999: 262), in future virtual reality we may be able to simulate and hence penetrate the real still further, and thus observe and reveal what has hitherto not yet been seen or known. It is not so much that virtual reality is the new frontier, since it is the real that the virtual allows us to explore, but it is certainly the most sophisticated medium invented for the interpretation of the real and for interaction with it.

Yet virtual reality should not be considered only as a medium to look into the future, but as a means to rewrite and reinterpret our past. This was beautifully and evocatively achieved in Tamás Waliczky's *The Forest* (1993). Here, the viewer is presented with an electronically reproduced forest of gigantic and barren black trees that are set against a white, slightly hazy background. The camera moves through the forest 'in a series of complex and melancholic moves' (Manovich 2001: 262) which have the effect of presenting the dichotomy between human subjectivity and computer logic.

> The camera system of *The Forest* foregrounds this double character of computer space [. . .] The constant movements of the camera along the vertical dimension throughout the film – sometimes getting closer to where we imagine the ground plane is located, sometimes moving toward (but

Figure 18 The Forest, Tamás Waliczky, © T. Waliczky and A. Szepesi, 1993–6.

again, never actually showing) the sky – can be interpreted as an attempt to negotiate between isotropic space and the space of human anthropology, with its horizontality of the ground space and the horizontal and vertical dimension of human bodies. The navigable space of *The Forest* thus mediates between human subjectivity and the very different and ultimately alien logic of a computer.

(Manovich 2001: 263)

The Forest exists in three separate versions: a computer animation, an interactive installation and a CD-ROM. The three versions present a number of similarities but are different in structure, although their common feature is 'the misty appearance of a black-and-white forest, stretching out in every direction as a symbol of hopeless searching' (Szepesi in Sommer 2002: 103). In the first version of *The Forest*, constructed as a computer animation, 'the image of the forest creates the impression of a three-dimensional space constructed from elements which themselves are only two-dimensional. The basis for the image is a black-and-white drawing of a bare tree.' Here, '[t]he effect of infinity is partly created by the suggestion of perpetual motion: to the viewer, the camera seems to move continually up and down in this endless forest which has no sky and no ground' (Szepesi in Sommer 2002: 108). The other two editions maintain this characteristic, and in all three, 'the camera, part of cinema's apparatus, becomes the main character' and the viewer is able to witness the fact that the whole film is 'one uninterrupted camera trajectory' (Manovich 2001: 262). While listening to the soundtrack, alternating what appears to be the sound of distant trains with the gentle lyrics of a female voice singing an old German children's song, perhaps hinting at the deportation and annihilation of hundreds of innocent children during the Holocaust, the viewer cannot help but lose themself, time and again, in this forest, which in its barrenness is so sadly resonant of all those deaths. The world of the forest is like a Limbo within which the viewer can do nothing but wait for something to happen. Here, it has been suggested,

> Waliczky's system of coordinates employs curved lines that loop back on themselves. This evokes a sense of limitless space: the viewer feels that there is no way out of the forest which extends in every direction. The bare trees revolve endlessly around their own axis, like patterns in a kaleidoscope. The resulting illusion is complete and deeply alarming: the infinity of the gaze leads to a total loss of perspective.
>
> (Szepesi in Sommer 2002: 109)

In this virtual environment, in which there are only traces of long-gone human beings and even nature has become barren and lifeless, there is nothing 'alive' but a camera which is in itself unable to create a narration. The viewer, caught in the work's circularity, becomes a mere witness of the emptiness produced by the horrors that have thus far attempted to destroy civilisation.

This art project, like many others discussed in this book, shows how virtual reality is being used as a means for the denunciation of the destruction, control and abuse that have repeatedly affected the modern world. In *The Forest*, the viewer is suspended, powerless, in an evocative space that could be a real space, a space of memory or the aftermath of the Apocalypse. What is so striking about this space is how much one can see within it, given that the work itself offers so little, if any, interaction. And this is the final major characteristic of virtual reality: by interfering with the viewer's sense of presence and imagination, it can, at least for a moment, remove them from the world they are in and allow them access to a different universe, one where a person could become another – and where everybody could ultimately enter that book, film, fairy-tale, landscape, galaxy, painting or atom that they had known of for such a long time and yet had never seen from within. This might be the space of virtual reality – a space where the real can be seen inside out.

BIBLIOGRAPHY

Aarseth, E. (1997) *Cybertext*, Baltimore, Md. and London: Johns Hopkins University Press.

Anon (1994) 'Art and Technology', *Art & Design*, 34, 33–87.

—— (2002) <http://www.telefonica.es/fat/eantunez.html> (accessed 4/11/2002).

Ascott, R. (ed.) (2000) *Art, Technology, Consciousness: mind@large*, Bristol: Intellect.

Auslander, P. (1997) *From Acting to Performance: Essays in Modernism and Postmodernism*, London and New York: Routledge.

—— (1999) *Liveness: Performance in a Mediatised Culture*, London and New York: Routledge.

Barthes, R. (2000) *Camera Lucida*, trans. R. Howard, London: Vintage.

Baudrillard, J. (1988) *The Ecstasy of Communication*, trans. B. Schutze and C. Schutze, New York: Semiotext(e).

—— (1993 [1983]) *Simulations*, trans. P. Foss, P. Patton and P. Beitchman, New York: Semiotext(e).

—— (1993 [1990]) *The Transparency of Evil, Essays on Extreme Phenomena*, trans. J. Benedict, London and New York: Verso.

—— (1994 [1981]) *Simulacra and Simulation*, trans. S. Fari Glaser, Ann Arbor, Mich.: University of Michigan Press.

—— (1995 [1991]) *The Gulf War Did Not Take Place*, trans. Power Institute and P. Patton, Sydney: Power Publications.

—— (1998 [1976]) *Symbolic Exchange and Death*, trans. I. Hamilton Grant, London: Sage Publications.

—— (1999) 'Photography, or the Writing of Light', trans. F. Debrix, CTHEORY, <http://www.ctheory.com/article/a83.html> (accessed 6/12/2000).

Baumgärtel, T. (2001) *[net.art 2.0] Neue Materiale zur Netzkunst/New Materials Towards Net Art*, Nuremberg: Verlag für moderne Kunst.

Becker, B. (2000) 'Cyborgs, Agents, and Transhumanists: Crossing Traditional Borders of Body and Identity in the Context of New Technology', *Leonardo*, 33: 5, 361–65.

Beckmann, J. (1998) *The Virtual Dimension*, New York: Princeton Architectural Press.

Bell, D. and Kennedy, B. (eds) (2000) *The Cybercultures Reader*, London and New York: Routledge.

Benedikt, M. (ed.) (1993 [1991]) *Cyberspace: First Steps*, Cambridge, Mass.: MIT Press.

Benjamin, W. (1992 [1955]) *Illuminations*, trans. H. Zohn, London: Fontana Press.

Blast Theory (2000) 'Desert Rain', <http: www.blastheory.easynet.co.uk/ work_desertrain_desc_body.html> (accessed 8/12/2000).

—— (2002) *Desert Rain*, catalogue.

Bolter, J. D. (1991) *Writing Space*, Hillsdale, NJ: Lawrence Erlbaum Associates.

Bolter, J. D. and Grusin, R. (2000) *Remediation: Understanding New Media*, 3rd edn, Cambridge, Mass.: MIT Press.

Borges, J. L. (1964) *Labyrinths: Selected Stories and Other Writings*, eds D. A. Yates and J. E. Irby, New York: New Directions.

Boyer, M. C. (1994) *The City of Collective Memory: Its Historical Imagery and Architectural Enhancements*, Cambridge, Mass.: MIT Press.

—— (1996) *Cybercities: Visual Perception in the Age of Electronic Communication*, New York: Princeton Architectural Press.

Burnham, J. (1968) *Beyond Modern Sculpture: The Effects of Science and Technology on the Sculpture of this Century*, London: Allen Lane/Penguin Press.

Burry, M. (ed.) (2001) *Cyberspace*, Victoria, Australia: Images Publishing Group.

Caplan, E. (1997) 'Dance on Film: Notes on the Making of CRWDSPCR', *Choreography and Dance*, 4: 30, 99–104.

Case, S.-E. (1995) 'Performing Lesbian in the Space of Technology: Part II', *Theatre Journal*, 47: 3, 5–10 and 329–43.

—— (1996) *The Domain-Matrix: Performing Lesbian at the End of Print Culture*, Bloomington and Indianapolis, Ind.: Indiana University Press.

Cavallaro, D. (2000) *Cyberpunk and Cyberculture*, London: Athlone Press.

Clarke, R. (2001) 'Reigning Territorial Plains – Blast Theory's "Desert Rain"', *Performance Research*, 6: 2, 43–50.

Copeland, R. (1999) 'Cunningham, Collage, and the Computer', *Performing Arts Journal*, 21: 3, 42–54.

Cubitt, S. (1991) *Timeshift: On Video Culture*, London and New York: Routledge.

Cuito, A. (ed.) (2000) *Ecological Architecture*, trans. R.-L. Rees, Barcelona: Loft Publications.

Cunningham, M. (1996) *CRWDSPCR*, video, Cunningham Dance Foundation.

DEAF95 (2002) <http://www.v2nl/DEAF/persona/roca.html> (accessed 4/11/2002).

De Landa, M. (1991) *War in the Age of Intelligent Machines*, New York: Zone Books.

Delany, P. and Landow, G. P. (eds) (1992) *Hypermedia and Literary Studies*, Cambridge, Mass.: MIT Press.

Deleuze, G. (1993) *The Fold*, trans. T. Conley, London: Athlone Press.

Deleuze, G. and Guattari, F. (1988; [1980]) *A Thousand Plateaus: Capitalism and Schizophrenia*, trans. B. Massumi, London: Athlone Press.

Dery, M. (1996) *Escape Velocity: Cyberculture at the End of the Century*, London: Hodder & Stoughton.

Dinkla, S. (1997) *Pioniere Interaktiver Kunst von 1970 bis heute*, Karlsruhe: Edition ZKM, Cantz Verlag.

Dixon, S. (1999) 'Remediating Theatre in a Digital Proscenium', *Digital Creativity*, 10: 3, 135–42.

Douglas, J. Yellowlees (1993) 'Where the Senses Become a Stage and Reading is Direction', *Drama Review*, 37: 4, 18–37.

Dreher, T. (2002) 'Artivismo: www.0100101110101101.ORG', <http://iasl.uni-muenchen.de/links/lektion11.html> (accessed 17/9/2002).

Druckrey, T. (ed.) (1996) *Electronic Culture: Technology and Visual Representation*, New York: Aperture.

Duguet, A.-M., Klotz, H. and Weibel, P. (1997) *Jeffrey Shaw – a User's Manual: From Expanded Cinema to Virtual Reality*, Karlsruhe: Edition ZKM, Cantz Verlag.

Etchells, T. (1999) 'Good Places Performance Photography, Imaginary Space', *Artintact*, 5, 53–63.

Featherstone, M. and Burrows, R. (1995) *Cyberspace, Cyberbodies, Cyberpunk*, London: Sage.

Fleischmann, M. (1995) <http://imk.gmd.de:8081/people/fleischmann.mhtml> (accessed 23/5/2001).

Forced Entertainment (1998a) *Paradise*, <http://www.lovebytes.org.uk/paradise/intro.html> (accessed 25/10/2002).

—— (1998b) *Nightwalks*, CD-ROM.

Franklin, S., Lury, C. and Stacey, J. (2000) *Global Nature, Global Culture*, London: Sage.

Frazer, J. (1995), 'The Architectural Relevance of Cyberspace', in 'Architects in Cyberspace', in *Architectural Design*, 65: 11/12, 76–81.

Gaggi, S. (1997) *From Text to Hypertext*, Philadelphia, Pa.: University of Pennsylvania Press.

—— (2000) 'The Body and its Limits', in *Degrés*, 101, section c, 1–24.

Galofaro, L. (1999) *Digital Eisenman*, Basel: Birkhäuser.

Gerbel, K. and Weibel, P. (eds) (1994) *Intelligente Ambiente. Intelligent Environments. Ars Electronica 1994*, Vienna: PVS Verleger.

Giannetti, C. (ed.) (1998) *Marcel-lí Antúnez Roca: Performances, objetos y dibujos*, Disseny: MECAD, Media Centre d'Art.

—— (ed.) (1999) *Marcel-lí Antúnez Roca: Epifanía*, Madrid: Fundación Telefónica.

Gibson, W. (1993 [1984]) *Neuromancer*, London: HarperCollins.

Glendinning, H., Etchells, T. and Forced Entertainment (2000) *Void Spaces*, Sheffield: Sheffield Site Gallery.

Goldberg, K. (ed.) (2000) *The Robot in the Garden: Telerobotics and Telepistemology in the Age of the Internet*, Cambridge, Mass.: MIT Press.

Gómez-Peña, G. (1996) <http://riceinfo.rice.edu/projects/CyberVato/> (accessed 17/2/2003).

—— (1998) <http://amsterdam.nettime.org/Lists-Archives/nettime-1-9805/msg00083.html> (accessed 17/2/2003).

—— (1999) 'Mexican Beasts, Holy Gang Members, & Webbacks: Activist Dioramas', *Theatre Forum*, 15, 53–7.

—— (2000) *Dangerous Border Crossers*, London and New York: Routledge.

Gray, C. H. (ed.) (1995) *The Cyborg Handbook*, London and New York: Routledge.

Gržinić, M. (2002) *Stelarc*, Ljubljana, Maribor: Maska MKC.

Haraway, D. (1991) *Simians, Cyborgs, and Women: The Reinvention of Nature*, London: Free Association Books.

Haraway, D. (1997) *Modest_Witness@Second_Millennium: FemaleMan©_Meets _Oncomouse™*, London and New York: Routledge.

Hayles, K. (1999) *How We Became Posthuman: Virtual Bodies in Cybernetics, Literature, and Informatics*, Chicago, Ill., and London: University of Chicago Press.

Heim, M. (1994) 'Nature and Cyberspace', *Doors of Perception CD-ROM*, Amsterdam: Mediamatic.

Hershman Leeson, L. (ed.) (1996) *Clicking In: Hot Links to a Digital Culture*, Seattle, Wash.: Bay Press.

Hershman L. (2003) <www.lynnhershman.com/> (accessed 5/2/2003).

Hübler, K. (1997) 'Knowbotic Research: Non-located Events: Interventions between the urban and the Electronic Environment', <www.canon.co.jp/cast/artlab/artlab7/lecture2.html> (accessed 6/1/2003).

Hünnekens, A. (1997) *Der bewegte Betrachter: Theorien der interaktiven Medienkunst*, Cologne: Wienand Verlag.

Imperiale, A. (2000) *New Flatness, Surface Tension in Digital Architecture*, Basel: Birkhäuser.

Ince, K. (2000) *Orlan: Millennial Female*, Oxford and New York: Berg.

Jacobson, L. (ed.) (1992) *CyberArts: Exploring Art and Technology*, San Francisco, Calif.: Miller Freeman Inc.

Jameson, F. (1991) *Postmodernism, or the Cultural Logic of Late Capitalism*, London: Verso.

Janko, S., Leopoldseder, H. and Stocker, G. (eds) (1996) *Ars Electronica Center Linz, Museum of the Future*, Linz: AEC Verein, Orf.

Johnson, L. (1993–4) 'Applications: LifeForms', *Dance Connection*, 2: 4, 27–30.

Kac, E. (1998) *Teleporting an Unknown State*, Maribor: Zbirka Edition.

—— (2002) <http://www.ekac.org> (accessed 2/12/2002).

Kaye, N. (1994) *Postmodernism and Performance*, Houndmills: Macmillan.

Keidan, L. (1996) *Totally Wired*, London: ICA.

Knowbotic Research (1997) *ArtLab7 10_DENCIES*, Tokyo: ArtLab.

—— (2003) <www.khm.de/people/krcf/> (accessed 6/1/2003).

Kostelanetz, R. (1994) *On Innovative Performance(s): Three Decades of Recollections on Alternative Theater*, Jefferson, NC, and London: McFarland.

Kostić, A. and Dobrila, P. T. (eds) (2000) *Eduardo Kac: Telepresence, Biotelematics, Transgenetic Art*, Ljubljana: Publication of the Association for Culture and Education.

Kozel, S. (1994a) 'Virtual Reality: Choreographing Cyberspace', *Dance Theater Journal*, 11: 2, 34–7.

—— (1994b) 'Spacemaker: Experiences of a Virtual Body', *Dance Theater Journal*, 11: 3, 12–13 and 46–7.

Krueger, M. (1991) *Artificial Reality II*, Reading, Mass.: Addison-Wesley Publishing Company.

Landow, G. P. (1989) 'Hypertext in Literary Education, Criticism and Scholarship', *Computers and the Humanities*, 23: 2, 173–98.

—— (1997) *Hypertext 2.0: The Convergence of Contemporary Critical Theory and Technology*, Baltimore, Md., and London: Johns Hopkins University Press.

Laurel, B. (1993) *Computers as Theatre*, New York, Bonn and Paris: Addison-Wesley.

Leeker, M. (ed.) (2001) *Maschinen, Medien, Performances: Theater and der Schnittstelle zu digitalen Welten*, Berlin: Alexander Verlag.

Leopoldseder, H. and Schöpf, C. (1999) *Cyber Arts 1999*, Vienna and London: Springer.

—— (2000) *Cyber Arts 2000*, Vienna and London: Springer.

Lévy, P. (1999 [1990]) *Les Technologies de l'Intelligence*, Paris: La Découverte.

—— (2001 [1997]) *Cyberculture*, trans. R. Bononno, Minneapolis, Minn. and London: University of Minnesota Press.

Lunenfeld, P. (2000) *Snap to Grid*, Cambridge, Mass.: MIT Press.

—— (2001) *The Digital Dialectic*, 3rd edn, Cambridge, Mass.: MIT Press.

Lyotard, J.-F. (1984; [1979]) *The Postmodern Condition: A Report on Knowledge*, trans. G. Bennington and B. Massumi, Manchester: Manchester University Press.

Manovich, L. (1995) 'The Aesthetics of Virtual Worlds', <http://www.nettime.org/desk-mirror/zkp2/virtual.html> (accessed 9/3/2002).

—— (2001) *The Language of New Media*, Cambridge, Mass.: MIT Press.

McCarthy, P. (1983) 'The Body Obsolete: Stelarc and Paul McCarthy Talk about the Power the Body Has over Itself', *High Performance*, 24, 14–19.

McCorquodale, D. (ed.) (1996) *Orlan: This Is My body . . . This Is My software . . .*, London: Black Dog Publishing.

McKenzie, J. (1994) 'Virtual Reality: Performance, Immersion, and the Thaw', *Drama Review*, 38: 4, 83–103.

McLuhan, M. (1987 [1964]) *Understanding Media: The Extensions of Man*, London: Art Paperbacks.

Merleau-Ponty, M. (1992 [1945]) *Phenomenology of Perception*, trans. C. Smith, London and New York: Routledge.

Mitchell, W. J. (1992) *The Reconfigured Eye: Visual Truth in the Post-Photographic Era*, Cambridge, Mass.: MIT Press.

Mitchell, W. (1999) *City of Bits*, Cambridge, Mass.: MIT Press.

Morse, M. (1998) *Virtualities*, Bloomington, Ind.: Indiana University Press.

Moser, M. A. and MacLeod, D. (eds) (1996) *Immersed in Technology*, Cambridge, Mass.: MIT Press.

Mulder, A. and Post, M. (2000) *Book for the Electronic Arts*, Rotterdam: De Balie.

Murray, J. H. (1999) *Hamlet on the Holodeck*, Cambridge, Mass.: MIT Press.

Novak, M. (1995) 'Transmitting Architecture', in 'Architects in Cyberspace', in *Architectural Design*, 65: 11/12, 43–7.

Oosterhuis, K. and Lénárd, I. (1998) *Kas Oosterhuis Architect, Ilona Lénárd Visual Artist*, Rotterdam: 010 Publishers.

Orlan (1997) *De L'Art charnel au baiser de l'artiste*, Paris: Éditions Jean-Michel Place.

Palumbo, M. L. (2000) *New Wombs: Electronic Bodies and Architectural Disorders*, Basel: Birkhäuser.

Perrella, S. (ed.) (1998) *Hypersurface Architecture*, London: Architectural Design.

—— (ed.) (1999) *Hypersurface Architecture II*, London: Architectural Design.

Phelan, P. (1993) *Unmarked: The Politics of Performance*, New York and London: Routledge.

Phelan, P. and Lane, J. (eds) (1998) *The Ends of Performance*, New York and London: New York University Press.

Popper, F. (1993) *Art of the Electronic Age*, London: Thames & Hudson.

Prestinenza Puglisi, L. (1999) *Hyper Architecture*, Basel: Birkhäuser.

Quick, A. (1999) 'Stills of the Night', *Performance Research: On Line*, 4: 2, 107–8.

Rabinow, P. (1992) 'Artificiality and Enlightenment: From Sociobiology to Biosociality', in Jonathan Crary and Sanford Kwinter (eds), *Incorporations*, New York: Zone, pp. 234–52.

—— (1996a) *Essays on Anthropology of Reason*, Berkeley, Calif.: University of California Press.

—— (1996b) *Making PCR: A Story of Biotechnology*, Chicago, Ill.: Chicago University Press.

Reynolds, D. (2000) 'Displacing "Humans": Merce Cunningham's Crowds', <www.brunel.ac.uk/depts/pfa/bstjournal/1no1/DEEreynolds.htm> (accessed 5/2/2003).

Robins, K. (1996) *Into the Image: Culture and Politics in the Field of Vision*, London and New York: Routledge.

Rush, M. (1999) *New Media in Late 20th-Century Art*, London: Thames & Hudson.

Saltz, D. Z. (2001) 'The Collaborative Subject: Telerobotic Performance and Identity', *Performance Research*, 6: 3, 70–83.

Schiphorst, T. (1997) 'Merce Cunningham: Making Dance with the Computer', *Choreography and Dance*, 4: 3, 79–98.

Schwartz, I. (1997) <http://www.archis.org/archis_art_e_1997/archis_art_9709_ENG.html> (accessed 5/12/2000).

BIBLIOGRAPHY

Schwarz, H.-P. (1997) *Medien-Kunst-Geschichte*, Münich and New York: Prestel.

Schwarz, H.-P. and Shaw, J. (1996) *Perspektiven der Medienkunst*, Karlsruhe: Edition ZKM, Cantz Verlag.

Sermon, P. (2003) <http://www.artdes.salford.ac.uk/sermon/vision/tv_a.html> (accessed 6/1/2003).

Shaw, J. (2002) <http://www.jeffrey-shaw.net/html_main/show_work.php3?record_id=94> (accessed 3/9/2002).

Sommer, A. (ed.) (2002) *The Complete Artintact vols 1–5 1994–9*, Karlsruhe: ZKM Hatje Cantz.

Sommerer, C. and Mignonneau, L. (1999) 'Art as a Living System: Interactive Computer Artworks', *Leonardo*, 32: 3, 165–73.

—— (2000) <http://www.mic.atr.co.jp/~christa> (accessed 6/12/2000).

—— (2001) 'Creating Artificial Life for Interactive Art and Entertainment', *Leonardo*, 34: 4, 303–7.

—— (eds) (1998) *Art @ Science*, Vienna and New York: Springer.

Sorkin, M. (1992) 'See You in Disneyland', in M. Sorkin (ed.) *Variations on a Theme Park: The New American City and the End of Public Space*, New York: Noonday.

Stelarc (1995) 'Toward the Posthuman', in *Architectural Design*, 65: 11/12, 91–6.

—— (1997) 'From Psycho to Cyber Strategies: Prosthetics, Robotics and Remote Experience', *Cultural Values*, 1: 2, 241–9.

—— (2002a) <http://www.stelarc.va.com.au> (accessed 12/4/2002).

—— (2002b) Interview with Gabriella Giannachi, Lancaster, 10 May.

Sterling, B. (1990) 'Cyberspace (TM)', *Interzone*, 41.

Steuer, J. (1992) 'Defining Virtual Reality: Dimensions Determining Telepresence', *Journal of Communications*, 42, 75–8.

Stocker, G. and Schöpf, C. (eds) (1996) *Memesis: The Future of Evolution, Ars Electronica 1996*, Vienna and New York: Springer.

—— (eds) (1997) *Flesh Factor: Ars Electronica 1997*, Vienna and New York: Springer.

—— (eds) (1998) *InfoWar: Ars Electronica 1998*, Vienna and New York: Springer.

—— (eds) (1999) *Life Science: Ars Electronica 1999*, Vienna and New York: Springer.

Stone, A. R. (1998 [1995]) *The War of Desire and Technology at the Close of the Mechanical Age*, Cambridge, Mass.: MIT Press.

Strathern, M. (1992a) *After Nature: English Kinship in the Late Twentieth Century*, Cambridge: Cambridge University Press.

—— (1992b) *Reproducing the Future: Anthropology, Kinship and the New Reproductive Technologies*, Manchester: Manchester University Press.

Sudjic, D. (1993) *The 100 Mile City*, London: Flamingo.

Turkle, S. (1995) *Life on the Screen*, London: Weidenfeld & Nicolson.

V2 (1997) *Technomorphica*, Rotterdam: Naj Publication.

—— (1998) *The Art of the Accident*, Rotterdam: Naj Publication.

Venturi, R. (1972) *Learning from Las Vegas*, Cambridge, Mass.: MIT Press.

Virilio, P. (1991; [1984]) *The Lost Dimension*, trans. D. Moshenberg, New York: Semiotext(e).

—— (1995) 'Speed and Information: Cyberspace Alarm', *CTHEORY*, <www.ctheory.com/article/a030.html> (accessed 24/10/01).

—— (1996 [1993]) *The Art of the Motor*, trans. J. Rose, Minneapolis, Minn. and London: University of Minnesota Press.

—— (1997 [1995]) *Open Sky*, trans. J. Rose, London and New York: Verso.

—— (2000) *Polar Inertia*, trans. P. Camillier, London: Sage.

Weibel, P. and Druckrey, T. (eds) (2001) *Net_condition: Art and Global Media*, Cambridge, Mass.: MIT Press.

Weibel, P. and Schmid, C. (eds) (2000) *Internationaler Medien/Kunstpresse*, Karlsruhe: ZKM.

Wertheim, M. (1999) *The Pearly Gates of Cyberspace*, London: Virago.

Wiener, N. (1948) *Cybernetics: Or Control and Communication in the Animal and the Machine*, New York: John Wiley.

Williams, R. (1980) 'Ideas of Nature', in *Problems in Materialism and Culture*, London: Verso.

Wilson, S. (2002) *Information Arts: Intersections of Art, Science, and Technology*, Cambridge, Mass.: MIT Press.

Wolford, L. (1999) 'The Politics of Identity in the United States of Aztlán: Pocha Nostra's *Mexterminator Project*', *Theatre Forum*, 15, 58–66.

Zellner, P. (1999) *Hybrid Space: New Forms in Digital Architecture*, London: Thames & Hudson.

0100101110101101.ORG (2002) <http://www. 0100101110101101.org/home/gui/about.html> (accessed 17/9/2002).

Zylinska, J. (2002) *The Cyborg Experiments: The Extensions of the Body in the Media Age*, London and New York: Continuum.

INDEX

INDEX

INDEX

INDEX